C0026 06727

D1152772

UNLICENSED

ie
ate,

MAINSTREAM SPORT

UNLICENSED

Random notes from boxing's underbelly

JON HOTTEN

MAINSTREAM
PUBLISHING

EDINBURGH AND LONDON

First published in Great Britain in 1998 by
MAINSTREAM PUBLISHING CO (EDINBURGH) LTD
7 Albany Street
Edinburgh
EH1 3UG

This edition 1999
Reprinted 2001

ISBN 1 84018 280 6

A CIP catalogue record for this book is available from the British Library

Typeset in Sabon
Printed and bound by Cox & Wyman Ltd, Reading, Berks.

For Simone
and GJC and MEM

'When we're in pursuit of fighting monsters, during that fight, we must make sure we don't become monsters'

Mike Tyson, quoting Friedrich Nietzsche
in *The Ring* magazine

CONTENTS

ACKNOWLEDGEMENTS

None of this would have been possible without the fighters, the boxing men. So John Barnwell, Mickey Sullivan, Billy Heaney, thank you, thank you for everything. Thanks also to Evander Holyfield, who was generous with his time, Mike Tyson and also the inimitable Don King. To Roy Shaw, thanks, too, and also to Brian Hills and Jimmy 'His Nibbs' Ryan.

Also, I am indebted to Ben Clissett, Mike Averis and all at the *Guardian* sports desk, Wayne Campbell, Gary Stephenson, Chris Haynes, Rachel Jeffries, Mick Wall, Paul Yelland, Derek Hammond, Armani Vance and Durban Poison Records, Bill Campbell, Peter MacKenzie, Cathy Mineards, Donald McRae and GiGi Dryer. Thanks go too to Julie Simpson and Michael Powell for the use of their houses . . .

Also, the Ghost of JCH, thank you.

Lily and Ruby, thank you. First, last and always, Simone. This one's for you, but you already knew that . . .

* * *

As the sub-title *Random Notes from Boxing's Underbelly* implies, this is not intended to be a definitive account of unlicensed fighting. It could not be. There are as many versions and varieties as there are fights and fighters. The nature of the game means that it is unregulated and cannot be catalogued, counted or assessed. Its edges are indistinct and its margins impossible to draw sharply. Neither is this a history of unlicensed fighting, nor does it set out to condone or condemn it. It merely reports on the parts of it that I saw. At the outset, there was no intention of including any professional boxing in this book, but it soon became obvious that the two worlds, licensed and unlicensed, were a part of the same whole, as the passage of events would prove.

Some of the names of the people in this book have been changed, the order of some events has been altered and some characters are amalgamations of two or more people. This has not been done to improve, distort or glamorise the book, but to respect the privacy and the lives of some of the people who helped. I hope that it does not alter the essential truths that lie behind this hard, hard game.

The Portuguese have a beautiful and melancholic word, *saudade*. It has no literal translation in English, but it means nostalgia for a time and place that never really existed. Like most of my generation of fight fans, I was drawn to boxing by two great eras: those of Muhammad Ali, 'Smokin'' Joe Frazier, George Foreman, Ken Norton and their contemporaries in the heavyweight division, and then the equally incandescent rivalries of 'Sugar' Ray Leonard, Roberto 'Hands of Stone' Duran, 'Marvellous' Marvin Hagler and Thomas 'The Hit Man' Hearns in the middleweight ranks. Even the nicknames were magical. No one could live through those days without an enduring admiration for any man who had the courage, heart and belief to enter the squared circle. There is no apology for the fact that that admiration extends to nearly everyone in this book. I hope it's obvious by the end why an apology is unnecessary.

CHAPTER ONE

A LONG LAST DAY FOR THE DOGMAN

The Dogman was waiting on the corner at one o'clock, as arranged.

'There he is, bang on time,' said Steve, as he steered the old transit down the wrong side of the road and stopped it right by his brother's feet.

The Dogman looked as big and as shabby as always in a loose brown leather coat – drug-dealer chic – and his sloppy black training pants. His baseball boots were white – once. His face wore its customary look of lopsided menace; the Dogman looked pissed off even when he wasn't. His eyes peered through thin and distrustful slits below a sloping forehead. He looked ugly and small-minded and his threat came naturally. None of this kept him awake at night.

He was tall, over six foot, and naturally rangy, and his long arms and legs swung from loose joints. The many hours he spent in the gym had added bulk to his tough sinew. He was twenty-five years old and known on these streets as a hard man, a tough nut not to be crossed, a cocky nutter whose eye was not worth catching.

Little kids sometimes followed him along when he left his council flat to walk his Jack Russells to the newsagent's, where he bought his copy of *The Sun* and his milk. They liked to be near him, as if they thought that some of his spirit might rub off on them.

Today was different, though. The devoted following had been shooed away. At the Dogman's feet, hunched like a mongrel pup, was his kit-bag, and in between his fingers was a cigarette, a rare departure from his strict training regime.

When the van pulled up, he picked up the kit-bag, flicked out the fag and stubbed it with a huge foot. He jumped in.

The Dogman swallowed up the space on the three front seats. He said nothing and looked implacable, like a black Clint Eastwood. His eyes were as thin as the watery sunshine leaking through the windscreen.

'Feel good, Dennis?' chirped up Steve. Dennis was the Dogman's real name.

The Dogman made no reply.

'That's good, that's good,' soothed Steve, apparently to me. 'See, 'e's mean as fuck now. Mean as fuck . . .' and he squealed his strangled little laugh.

We drove mostly in silence out to the edges of the urban sprawl where London stopped being a city and began to flatten out and spread towards the coasts of Kent and Essex. Steve guided the van and made stabs at conversation as we slipped easily along. Soon we were switching through side streets and then on to back alleys and through arches, and then behind deserted offices and storerooms, and then on to a patch of derelict ground that used to be a car park. We were melting from view. There were some faint white lines that had once marked the bays, but the cars were long gone. Weeds poked up through the cracks and holes, and out at the edges the concrete began to curl up like a bad carpet. Steve stopped at a spot where two cars were parked up and he and I jumped out. The Dogman stayed put. Even Steve didn't bother with a goodbye.

'Good sign, when he's like that,' he muttered, almost to himself. It was becoming Steve's mantra.

At the far end of the wasteland, edged by a rusting chain-link fence the colour of dirt, was a warehouse. It was not the sort of place you could stumble on; whatever had once been here was years gone. There was no reason to visit it by accident, especially on a downbeat, quiet, summer Sunday afternoon like this one. It was an abandoned place, a place you might live next to for decades and yet never once explore. It was a small urban black hole. Nearby there were streets, houses, shops; nearby there was life. But here there was nothing of note. The weather was grey and then bright, grey and then bright, as unsure and ambivalent as the business of the afternoon.

I fingered the square card in my pocket. It was orange and had sketches of a car and a champagne bottle with the cork flying out printed on it, and a stencilled number '71' in one corner. It had cost me a tenner from a man called Big Mick Peters, who had promised me 'a good show; we've got a big paddy fighting his bollocks off against a top blackie' . . .

Big Mick had parted with the orange ticket after some persuasion and with the identity of the 'top blackie' after even more. Mick's show was not for widespread consumption. He had sold about twenty tickets to his acquaintances, and had passed thirty or so others to the fighters themselves, so we were a select crew. Mick charged the Dogman and Paddy a fiver each for their allocation, allowing them to pocket the mark-up on every ticket that they sold.

* * *

Mick had pointed the Dogman out to me across the pub a few nights after he had sold me a ticket. He was leaning on the bar in a Chicago Bulls vest and the ever-present black sweatpants. He worked as a doorman across the pubs and clubs on his patch. The 'Dogman' nickname came about, Mick explained, after Dennis took a fight with a pit-bull terrier and won it at the price of having one hand mangled in the mutt's heavy jaws, which had to be prized apart even after it was dead. At the time it seemed like an inconceivable piece of urban mythology, but it was a match I was to hear about again as the edges between professional boxing and unlicensed boxing and back-room fighting and sheer street savagery blurred. Every man drew his line in a different place, and there were plenty who saw man against dog as a watchable scrap. As someone would later maintain, with supremely twisted logic, it was fairer than a bullfight.

Dennis the Dogman had sometimes settled his grudges with fist fights in pub back rooms and in quiet parks and backstreets, and men would pay to watch. He could punch hard and he was pitiless and quick to the finish. The fights, Mick said, didn't usually last long, so he'd set up the scrap with Paddy.

Dennis was willing, anxious even, to extend his reputation as a streetfighter, an unlicensed man. He had heard that good men could make big money fighting in this way, and so had I.

'He thinks it will be easy,' Mick told me. 'He thinks Paddy will just go down like these blokes from the pub, but he won't. Dennis is going to find out what it's about. It's the only way to see if he's any cop.' Mick sounded like a man who'd picked up a few shares in ICI, a small investment, to see if they were worthy of any more of his efforts.

* * *

Big Mick was waiting at the door of the warehouse, which was nothing more than a wide gap in the side of the building. He was standing with two other men, both white, each with close-cropped hair and the black puffa bomber jackets beloved of doormen everywhere. He nodded to me and Little Steve.

'All right,' he mumbled, almost imperceptibly, and motioned us through.

'Yeah, all right. Thanks.'

Inside the warehouse it became obvious why the fight was on a summer's afternoon. The only light sources were natural ones, from the doors at either end and from the holes for two fire doors, one at each side, and also from six skylights that had all had the glass smashed out or stolen. Every time the sun broke through the clouds outside, great columns of light beamed down from the ceiling, filled with circling motes of dust. It was strangely sepulchral inside; it felt almost like a film set, half-contrived, not for realism but to add to the atmosphere.

In the centre of the floor, a rough and temporary ring had been put up. It had short scaffold poles for corner-posts, all unpadded, with bases that had been knocked together by a welder long ago to keep them upright. Each pole had two hooks on its inside that allowed the ropes to be threaded through. One rope was blue, the other white, and they were not proper ring ropes but more the sort that had been lifted from a building site. There was no matting on the floor, so it would be a hard fall for anyone who hit the deck.

Around the ring, fight fans had already begun to gather. They were easy to split into the camps of each of the contenders. The 'big paddy fighting his bollocks off' had the majority of them, mostly hard cases in casual clothes.

Men arrived in dribs and drabs over the next half an hour, just as Mick Peters had planned. He didn't want fifty people arriving at a place like this at the same time. They gravitated towards the ring and soon the occasional breezes that blew through the warehouse felt good in the tightening air. There seemed to be little tension between the fans of Paddy and the Dogman, but there was a vague sense of unease about the anticipation.

From the holes at the rear of the building came three men: Paddy, his second and one other. Paddy was an incongruous shape for a fighter. His head was bald, so instead he sported a grey goatee beard. His skin was going the same colourless way, sallow and loose around his jawline. He looked George Foreman's forty-eight and then some. He wore a hooded top that was stretched tight across his beer gut. The sleeves were hacked off around his meaty forearms. He too had old black sweatpants on, and a pair of discoloured boxing boots that he'd laced over the top of his trousers. His gloves were dark brown and heavily taped at his wrists. He pushed his way to his corner, where his second dumped a black bucket filled with water.

Then, from the same back door, came Dennis the Dogman. For Paddy's benefit, or maybe for his own mental well-being, he had already pulled off his training top to reveal his broad shoulders and thick chest, his fine condition. He wore his sweatpants and boxing boots.

Dennis's mouth had developed a bit of a twitch in the short time we'd been apart. He kept chewing on the inside of his cheek and his eyes were locked in a thousand-yard stare.

Steve came and stood next to me. He was fidgety and tense too. 'Cor, he looks fit, he looks good, dunne?' he muttered. I didn't reply. It was plain that Dennis the Dogman was feeling the occasion. This was no grudge match, no pub flare-up or handing-out of doorman's justice. This was a cold-start fight, a real fight. A test. And Dennis had rarely been tested.

Both men were accompanied by shouts of support. 'Fucking hammer him, Paddy,' one yelled, leading to a welter of shouts and counter-shouts.

Big Mick had materialised in the centre of the ring. He was both referee and judge. A timekeeper had brought a hand-held bell to sound the rounds. The fight had been set at four two-minute sessions, no kicking, butting, gouging, biting or rough-housing. Big Mick was firm about that. He would, he said, have them broken up and taken out if they tried it, and he nodded in the direction of several big and uncompromising men who lined one side of the ring. The atmosphere had lifted, notch by notch, to this point. My stomach turned over. I found myself feeling like I did before any big fight, excited by the inevitably unequivocal outcome, on edge with the immediacy, the danger and the unknown.

The bell sounded and Paddy and the Dogman cracked together. Dennis swung, huge and random swings aimed to take advantage of his reach. Paddy, though, had obviously done a bit in the ring. He moved away from them easily enough, although he wasn't light on his feet and slid in towards the Dogman, cutting the distance between them down. Paddy's punches came short and straight, and when he wasn't punching he kept his hands up and his chin down. He could box, and he was tough.

The Dogman threw another right hand, and this time Paddy didn't see it coming. It whistled into the side of his head, just above his ear.

'Yeeesss . . .' went Little Steve, and he jumped in the air.

It was a juddering shot but Paddy swallowed it with aplomb. His torso swung heavily to one side, but his legs showed no signs of betraying him. That, more than anything that was to follow, finished the Dogman. Outside of the ring, on the door of the nightclub, on the streets, the people he hit went down and stayed down. Here was a man who took his best shot and then moved towards him to land a punch of his own. Dennis lacked the skill to follow through with a second heavy blow, as a good fighter would by second nature. His brain stripped its gears almost audibly. He grabbed Paddy with his long arms and held on, spoiling for the bell, which soon came, his ambition shrinking towards survival alone.

Paddy took a faceful of cold water from the black bucket, and Dennis did the same. The Irishman stood with his arms spread across the top rope either side of his corner. He looked relaxed and calm. The Dogman didn't. His chest rose and fell as he pulled at the air. He couldn't stand still and he wasn't listening to the advice he was getting, good advice about keeping his chin down and his arms up and about not sending a telegram with every round-arm swing.

The handbell sounded for the second and then the third. They were bad times for the Dogman, among the worst times. In front of the men he'd sold tickets to, who had money riding on his sleek viciousness, and in front of his silent and sad little brother, he was taken apart by a fat old paddy. Dennis and Steve and I were learning a lesson about the unlicensed game. As the heat from the men overcame the breeze blowing through the warehouse, we attended a school of violence for the uneducated. As Paddy's punches thudded home in a hard rain, the effort barely raising colour on his big, still-grey face, he proved that a fight is about more than menace and appearances, about more than flooring men in pubs, about more than being muscular and terrifying and killing pit-bulls. The reputation of the Dogman was being dismantled by a forty-eight-year-old who could take a shot and hit back, who could move out of the way and deliver blows with technique as well as bad intentions behind them.

As we were standing close enough to hear the punches landing with their soft, deceptive thuds, the sensations were stripped barer than they were at the professional shows. At the pro fights, the contests carried a sheen of unreality that was not present here. Here, the punches sounded like punches, complete with the suckings of breath and the snorts of pain and surprise as they landed. There was an implacability to the fight, a veneer of violence of the purest strain.

Paddy threw a casual right cross and it skimmed the end of Dennis's nose, catching it a glancing blow as it scudded past. Small bullets of blood followed in the punch's wake and some of them landed on the shirts of me and Little Steve. Steve

23

looked down almost in disbelief at this light, red rain. The round ended.

The Dogman answered the bell for the last, crossing the ring with a view to taking the centre from Paddy. He did, but it cut his odds no shorter. Paddy swung slowly and steadily, an old dog with old tricks. He took Dennis's hands down with some heavy shots to the kidneys and then went back to work on his head. The Dogman's thin eyes were slipping behind the puffy hoods of his brows. His efforts to defend himself grew vaguer, less determined and decisive.

Paddy sucked in his breath and landed a big right, swung from way back. The Dogman didn't see it and it landed on his temple in an accelerating downward arc. He blinked hard and his knees dropped from underneath him as he crumpled down on top of himself. He looked grey now, as grey as Paddy, and sicker. Big Mick pulled him up and held on to him. Dennis's big arms drooped on his shoulders. They stayed like that for maybe fifteen seconds as the small crowd around the ring shouted and called. Little Steve looked away. Mick Peters moved back and Dennis sagged again, still out on his feet. The bell rang almost as he hit the concrete.

There was no need for Mick to raise Paddy's hand, and Paddy felt no need to do it himself. He didn't spare Dennis as much as a glance as he stepped out between the ropes. He simply walked away, unconcerned, untroubled and unsurprised.

Dennis the Dogman came round slowly, dopily, the aura he'd carried into the ring gone, along with the sunshine and the columns of light that had fallen in through the ceiling but were now banished by the clouds. The men who'd paid to see his fall were off and away even before his senses cleared again. Reality for the Dogman was going to be a hard thing to come back to.

The men watching, or at least those on the Dogman's side, were first quietened and then resigned. If they hurt for their man or for their cash, they didn't show it much. The edge to the atmosphere had flopped as badly as Dennis. They just turned away and went home.

'A good four rounds, that,' Big Mick grunted happily as we walked out of the big door spaces and back into the warehouse car park. 'Paddy's a good man, see. A fucking hard man. He's worth his money.'

Mick and Paddy met over by the rusty fence and Mick handed over his cash. Paddy's second had already pulled off his gloves and thrown them into a bag, along with his tapes.

'Good fight, Paddy,' I managed to muster.

'Too easy, son,' he smiled. 'Too easy . . .'

Paddy pulled a sweatshirt on, and then, with a nod, was gone, victorious, in a builder's van. Mick got into his car. I walked back through the warehouse and looked around the back, but Steve and Dennis had left too. Ten minutes after the fight, and everything and everyone had gone.

It had begun to rain more steadily, cold drops in the humid air that landed and quickly darkened the pavements. I looked at them, and at the burgundy-coloured drops of blood-rain on my shirt.

Like the old song says, it felt like it was raining all over the world.

CHAPTER TWO

MEETING MONSTERS

Danny's gym was a fighter's place, no doubt about it. It was in the cellar under a pub called the Black Cap on the corner of two streets in south-east London. It was not the sort of boozer that the brewery would bother renovating. It would never become an 'American' pool hall or a steak house. It had the decay of the years on it, on the mulchy carpets and chipped tables. The punters were a hard crowd who drank unfashionable beer.

There was no sign anywhere to indicate that Danny's gym even existed, either out on the street or inside the pub.

'Is there a boxing gym round here?' I asked the Irish kid who was serving the drinks.

'No, mate, I don't think there is . . .'

I went back out on to the street. The Black Cap was a big

old pub, with three bars and about five entrances. I walked around for a while, and rechecked the directions that were scribbled on the back of an envelope from a gas bill. The Black Cap was definitely the place.

Danny's gym was well hidden. When you walked through the street door from the main road, there was another set of double doors in front of you that opened into the pub. To the left was an old door wedged half-open and behind it some uneven concrete steps that doubled back on themselves halfway down. The air was damp. Lining the walls were peeling fight posters, mostly for local heroes long forgotten by everyone except the boxing *cognoscenti*. But by the time I saw the posters, I already knew that it was the right place. The smell of the gym, the grunts and snorts and barks of breath, and the noise of the punch bags bouncing on their chains all marked it out.

It was a fighter's place for sure, stripped of frills. The floors and walls were uneven cellar concrete painted with cheap white matt paint. The gym was divided into two rooms. The back section had a couple of bags and a speedball and some old mats on the floor. The near room had the heavy bag, a couple of medium bags and a two-rope ring that lay at floor level. It had mats for canvas and corner-posts that sagged backwards and could barely hold the ropes tight. To the side of the ring was an old wooden bench so the trainers could sit and watch. On the wall above was a timer clock to mark the rounds of sparring. One revolution of the hand took four minutes. The first three, marked in blue, were for the round. The fourth, in red, was the break. A buzzer sounded to mark the end of three minutes, and also the end of four.

There was a small office immediately to the right of the

entrance to Danny's. It had a stable door on it, with the bottom half shut. Danny sat inside on a bar stool. He was a tall, sinewy black man with a wild shock of hair. He eyed every entrant with suspicion.

I was at the gym to meet a man called John Barnwell. Maybe Danny would know him?

'Who?' he asked, obviously irritated.

'Is John Barnwell here?'

'Never heard of him.' The evening was already beginning to prove difficult. Apparently no one at the Black Cap or at Danny's knew anything.

'I spoke to him on the phone. He told me I could meet him here tonight.'

'John Barnwell?' Danny said, mouthing the name as if it was in a foreign language. 'Never heard of him. Who's asking?'

He left his little office and crossed the gym. He disappeared into another room for a while. Eventually he came back.

'What did you say your name was again?'

Some of the other fighters in the gym were staring over. It was unsettling.

'All right,' Danny relented. 'He said he'll see you. He's in the back. Go through.' He smiled, exposing a row of immaculate teeth. He gestured towards the small room that he had just emerged from.

The space was like a tiny stone cave. It was filled with steam that was coming from a small shower. Two men sat on a narrow bench, with towels wrapped around their midriffs.

The man on the left looked up.

'I'm John Barnwell.'

He was a man mountain. He had snow-white, straight hair, neatly parted above his big face. Beneath his broad neck, his shoulders sloped outwards endlessly. He had a barrel chest and a big, protruding stomach. He was forty-eight years old. When we shook hands, his huge paw swallowed mine and crushed down on my fingers. He eyed me up and down.

'I'm just 'aving a st . . steam,' he said. He spoke with a slight stammer. 'I'll . . . I'll see you upstairs in ten minutes. I'll have a Guinness with a bit of blackcurrant in the top.'

* * *

I sat in the pub and waited for half an hour, perched next to John's Guinness. The time dragged like a long exam, a test. Then he came in, holding an old black bag with his kit in. He took a couple of good pulls on the Guinness and we started to talk.

I had been told about John by a friend who trained at Danny's gym with his brother. The brother was just about to go pro. He had heard that John was involved in unlicensed fighting and that he might be willing to talk for a newspaper piece that I was trying to put together.

He said nothing at all while I blathered on about not naming names and turning over all my interview tapes to him and anything else I thought he might like to hear.

He blinked hard before he spoke. It was a little nervous tic he had. 'Yeah, yeah . . . It might be all right, like.'

John slowly became more at ease. Boxing proved good common ground. He liked the fighters who mixed it in the ring: Danny McAlinden and Jack Bodell, Alan Minter and 'Marvellous' Marvin Hagler, James 'Lights Out' Toney and Iron Mike Tyson. Slowly, John told a little of his own story. He was from

Coventry and he'd first walked into a gym when he was eleven years old, mainly because it seemed like he had something about him that other people wanted to fight. He had always been big for his age, but he soon discovered that he was skilful too, with a natural aptitude for the cunning of the ring and for the study of its pain-lessening techniques. His size lent weight to his naturally heavy punch.

He trained in the same gym as his hero Danny McAlinden for a while. John fought as an amateur in the days when it was a spectacle, before the gap between the three-round distance and the pros grew vast, and sometimes he would fight five times in a day.

It quickly became obvious that John's life was entwined around boxing, both licensed and unlicensed. He was still registered as a trainer by the British Boxing Board of Control, which made him cautious about discussing his involvement with the unlicensed game.

He drank another pint of Guinness with blackcurrant in. The more talkative he became, the less he stammered.

'If you look at me, you might think, "Oh, he's just a big fat prat." But I can fight, see? Most of 'em that you meet, they're just bar-room heroes. They don't understand how hard it is to fight. And if you know a bit, you can keep out of trouble. They go mad in the first round, try to knock you out. Keep out of trouble, that's all you have to do. Keep your head, keep nice and cool. Even the first round they're gonna wear themselves out so much trying to knock you out. The bigger they come, the less stamina they've got. The second round comes and their mouths are open. Give it another round; after that, they're just takeable.'

I told John about the Dogman. It was the extent of my

experience in unlicensed fighting and all that was on offer in terms of credentials. He just shrugged. It was small-time stuff, a few men watching a predictable scrap.

'I'll get Mickey to pop up,' he said suddenly. 'He's had a few fights, you know, unlicensed, like.' He nearly always ended his sentences with a 'like' hanging in the air.

Mickey came and sat with John. His name was Mick Sullivan. He was from Streatham Hill and he'd been coming to Danny's for twelve years. He had a heavyweight's physique, broad shoulders and a tapered waist and shaved-to-the-scalp, prematurely grey hair. He had taken fifteen fights as an un-licensed heavyweight and won all but two. Seen up close, his face was delicately boned. It looked too fragile to mix it in the ring, but his pug nose told another story.

'I lost a couple, close decisions. One on a cut,' he said. 'Sometimes it's hard to judge a fight that's four rounds.'

Mickey liked Guinness with a drop of blackcurrant in the top too. Some more drinks came. Mickey began to talk about his first fight in the unlicensed game.

'Somebody just offered it to me,' he said. 'It was over in east London somewhere, in a warehouse. I just accepted it. He offered me six hundred quid, I think.'

'How did you feel?'

'Yeah, I was nervous, but you don't show it.'

'When you're fighting the heavyweights, they can come my size, or even bigger,' John interjected. I looked at him again. I guessed that he weighed at least nineteen stone, which turned out to be a pretty fair guess.

'Had you seen him before the fight?' I asked Mickey.

'I'd caught a glimpse of him. He was big. It was lucky enough I could keep mobile. I stopped him in the last round.'

'Keep out of trouble, like I said,' John remarked.

'Yeah. This bloke, stopped him fourth round,' Mickey continued. 'He was swinging for three rounds, then I caught him with a right hand.'

'He was a nutter, wasn't he?' said John, trying to remember exactly who it was that Mickey had fought. 'Yeah, he wasn't that gypsy, he was the one who turned up in Maidstone? He was fighting that Davey Whitling. Davey stopped him that night.'

'Yeah, anyway, you're in the game then,' said Mickey, ignoring John's digression. 'When I'd won the fight, a guy came up to me and made the challenge. He said, "Fight me next time." He just jumped up. He had all his mates ringside, see.'

'Well, you get challenges, you see, different doormen will have a go at you,' John confirmed. 'They're all sort of pissed. All their mates going, "You could have him," so they'll say, "Me and you next." Like that gypsy nutter, or whoever he was.'

John's way took a while to get used to. He remembered things in great rushes, as if he was pulling them back from a long way away. Mixed with his stammer, it meant that you had to be patient to get the best of his stories. It gave him a vulnerable quality, even with his vast size.

Danny locked up the gym at about nine, and he came upstairs and joined us. Danny had been a pro fighter, a long, lean middleweight whose speed made him a tricky proposition.

'I was good as a pro,' he told me. John nodded his agreement. 'I lasted three fights as a pro and I didn't lose. If I could get away with taking a couple of fights unlicensed now, I would, but too many people know my face.'

We talked until closing time. John and Mickey were good

company, even though it seemed that their lives had been shot through with a violence that I could only begin to imagine.

They trained at Danny's every Tuesday and Thursday. Every week, I'd go down to the gym and sit on the narrow bench by the ring while John and Mickey went two or three rounds, and then they'd drink at one of the small tables in the Black Cap's long bar. John explained the rudiments of unlicensed boxing to me. It had many shapes and it occupied a grey area of the law. In its rawest form, as bare-knuckle streetfighting, it was wholly illegal. In its most refined, where the fights were with gloves and timed rounds and judges, it featured trained competitors who did not hold licences issued by the British Boxing Board of Control.

In and around London, anyone acquainted with gym culture could find a scrap most weekends. And that was just London. Beyond that there was the north, there was Europe and there was America, and probably anywhere where men fought in an organised fashion, fights without number. Because it was un-regulated, it was impossible to catalogue or historicise, to count or assess. Its edges were blurred, its margins ill-defined.

* * *

John and Mickey and I became friends over the nights in the Black Cap after training. Parts of John's remarkable life began to emerge, usually in random fashion. He was a raconteur when he loosened up, and his tales would undergo huge digressions as he remembered funny little incidents and long, strange nights. I began to see exactly how closely the worlds of licensed and unlicensed fighting existed. They slid together and then separated, subtly entwined. John had worked as a trainer and a cornerman for many years. He had been close to Alan Minter's manager, Doug Bidwell, and he had helped to train Minter out in Spain for a couple of his fights. At the same time, he had taken on men from all over the world in the unlicensed game.

'I was gonna go over to, er, Turkey,' he told me. 'That would have been good money. You get your purse plus a share of the door. That would be good money. They pay your flight, all your expenses. Take two blokes with you. The actual purse was six, seven grand, but you get door money too.' He stopped to take a drag on his Guinness.

'I saw the Turkish bloke fight someone else, a German bloke. He was a great big bloke, but slow. If he catches you, you've had it.'

I tried to keep John on track with the story of the fight against the Turk, but he was off.

'There's a big bloke come down here, he was six foot five, maybe twenty-three, twenty-five stone, but he was no good. He hit me on top of the head. My legs went. He weren't hard, he was nothing. You caught him with one good punch, he'd go, "Hang about." Couldn't take the pain. You shouldn't tell anybody they've hurt you. If somebody hits you hard, you got to swallow it. If your legs go, your hands go, he'll go straight for you. If you take a punch, you must throw one back. If not, he'll come in. If he's intelligent enough. Won't stop till the ambulance comes. You hang on, and you don't let go. Let the ref drag you off. It only takes one punch, no matter who you are.'

Driving home that night, I wondered what sort of punch it would take to fell a man like John, what sort of damage it would wreak and what sort of man might be able to throw it. On the quiet roads, as the car hummed along, the unlicensed game appeared to be a dark and impenetrable world, haunted by monsters.

* * *

John had asked me to come down to the gym early. He wanted me to meet a fighter whom he trained, to watch his man spar a few rounds. John had told me something about him and, despite my reservations, I was excited by what I'd heard. He was known as Billy Heaney, but that wasn't his real name. His nickname, which I had a suspicion had been dreamed up by John over a couple of drinks in the Black Cap, was the 'Galway Bull'. He sounded too good to be true, a real-life Rocky Balboa, a man from the street who could rise up and beat anyone, a gym legend who lived to fight, who came alive in the violence.

Nearly every gym has stories around it like this, about fighters who could be a Hagler or a Eubank if they had half a chance, but John and Mickey Sullivan spoke of Billy with awe. The first inkling as to why came when he walked in.

He was only five foot seven inches tall, but he weighed seventeen stone. His neck disappeared into his shoulders before it had even begun. His build made him a white Tyson, thickset with a naturally low centre of gravity. It was the classic puncher's body. Billy's nose snaked around his face like a ring road and he had ruddy cheeks from his day job, which was digging holes in the roads for pipes and TV cables. He wore an old blue shell-suit and trainers without socks. John swapped his bag gloves for a pair to spar in. Mickey Sullivan was already in Danny's sagging ring.

I went and sat on the thin, hard bench at ringside, close enough to put my hands through the tired old ropes. Mickey paced across the mat as he waited for the timer on the clock to tick around. He kept shifting his gumshield around his mouth and fiddling with his headguard. The buzzer sounded and Mickey leant out towards Billy and kept him away with his long jab. Billy stayed back for a while but then began to walk through the punches, cutting down the space between him and Mickey and bringing his own shots up from low down. Billy was snorting and bulling forwards, using his weight to push Mickey on to the ropes. He squared Mickey up right in front of me and began to unload sweet, short-arm body shots from both hands. It looked so simple, almost gentle, but it was the opposite. The punches bounced off Mickey's elbows and sides. The ones to his ribs echoed. They sounded like someone tapping a microphone. Mickey was a hard man, but he looked ready to fold. The sweat flew off him as he lost a little colour in his cheeks. John Barnwell called a halt. Mickey's face was pinched tight with pain. He leant against the top rope for almost a minute with his head bowed before he walked over to Billy and touched his gloves. He pulled his gumshield out and said to me, 'Not too bad tonight. He took it quite easy . . .'

* * *

It was a thrill to watch him punch. I'd seen some big boys up close – Tyson, Holyfield, Moorer – and Billy's shots were as pitiless as theirs. He was what John called a perfect puncher, someone whose body had, by happy accident, knitted together in such a way that power flowed through it from the tips of his toes dug in the canvas to his knuckles buried in his gloves. He lacked the hand speed, lateral movement and ring mobility of a good pro fighter, but he had a warrior's heart and he could certainly hit.

Most of what I learned about him came from John and Mickey. He was born in Galway into a large family. Until he came to England when he was fifteen, he spoke mainly in a local dialect of Gaelic. He was a gypsy bare-fist champion at fourteen, boxing out of doors in the traditional Romany way. He found work as a doorman in Brixton, and worked a door on his own before he turned sixteen. He could handle anyone from the streets. He retained the bare-fist title at sixteen, twenty-one and twenty-four. The only time he was ever beaten up, John said, was when he returned to Galway for a bare-fist fight, which he won easily. Before he could put his shirt back on, the gypsy women surrounded him and beat him on the bare back with the heels of their shoes, leaving him badly cut.

He had begun to go to the gym to keep in shape, and the fights started to come. John found him in the ring at Danny's when he was twenty-six years old.

'When I first met Billy, the old bloke was downstairs, Eddie. It was a brawl . . . Oh, God. Billy's the only guy who's ever knocked me down. Billy's knocked me down straight four or five times. Cracking punches. He hit me once, I thought he'd done my nose. You don't know you've gone down. I got up, all that feeling round there.' He gestured to his nose and lips. 'I said, "Where did you catch me? On the nose?" He said, "No, on the forehead."'

'He was a perfect puncher, absolutely natural. If I'd had him when he was twenty-one and he had turned pro, I would have put him in with any heavyweight in the country.'

Billy barely spoke at all. He was shy and modest, but friendly. He had personal reasons for not wanting to talk at any length, but he was happy for John to pass on what I wanted to know.

He still worked a door as well as digging roads. The place he looked after had a video called *Billy's Greatest Hits*, filmed on the closed-circuit camera that showed him sorting out unruly entrants. Sometimes the landlord would show it on the pub's video screen, much to everyone's delight.

He had money and owned several properties in London, which he rented out, and he had built a large holiday home over the Irish Sea. John had taken the money across to Ireland for him. He had a BMW and several other cars. He had made a considerable amount from fighting, but most of it came from the digging. Billy was the fastest, hardest digger around, and he got paid by the yard. He dug a lot of yards.

He was so quiet and unassuming that if I hadn't seen his talent from the ringside, his pre-eminence might have been hard to believe. But the more people spoke of him, the more it became obvious that he was an unlicensed hero, a dark star talked of with reverence.

* * *

Billy would never drink in the Black Cap. It was something to do with the complicated politics of which doormen went in which pubs, so I would spend my time in the cellar at Danny's leaning over the ropes after he'd finished sparring, trying to tease more than a smile out of him.

'The quiet ones are the worst,' John said. 'If it weren't for his nose, you wouldn't think anything of him. You'd think he was a fat Irish prat. But you'd come unstuck. Christ Almighty! He broke three of my ribs last year.'

'Is he the best unlicensed guy you've seen?'

'Pound for pound the best,' John agreed. And then he added, in another of his little digressions, 'He's coming down. He's about eighteen and a half, nineteen stone. He eats a lot.'

'But like Tyson's born to fight, Billy's born to fight. He's made for it,' said Mickey. Mickey thought Billy's style most resembled Oscar Bonevena's.

There was another story doing the rounds at Danny's about Billy. A world-famous British heavyweight, who was later to become a highly regarded world champion, dropped in one day looking for some sparring. John and Billy were there. Billy volunteered to have a 'walk around' – that was what the trainers referred to as a gentle workout. John told Billy that he would pull him out as soon as the session became too much. In the first three minutes, Billy was slaughtered. John was on the verge of stepping in. Then the buzzer sounded.

'I'm pulling you out,' John told Billy.

'No,' said Billy. 'He can't punch. I'm all right.'

The second round started and Billy unloaded with a big shot. The champ called a halt to the sparring right away, claiming he was not fit enough yet. He had tasted Billy's power and he didn't fancy any more. John swore the story was true, and Billy nodded when I asked him about it. It seemed like a tall gym tale, but then I thought again about how hard he could punch . . .

* * *

John and Mickey Sullivan brought some videos to the gym. One was a collection of fights from the 1970s that Mickey had put together. Part of it featured an underground film called *The Guv'nor*, about a brawler called Roy Shaw, otherwise known as 'Pretty Boy'. Shaw was a legend of the unlicensed game, in the ring and on the streets. The film was shot in the raw, on video camera, and this was a copy a couple of generations old. There was no voiceover, just some music, an overdub of Bruce Springsteen's 'Jungleland' from the *Born to Run* album.

The first fight on the tape was a fable of the underground – 'Pretty Boy' Shaw versus Donny 'The Bull' Adams. It was put on in front of a large audience in a circus tent. Shaw looked far more like a Bull than Adams, who was an ageing gypsy fighter. Shaw was short, squat and muscular. On the bell he threw a straight right into the face of Adams and put him down. Adams slumped into a corner. Shaw walloped him twice more and then attempted to lift him up so that he could continue to fight. The referee was yelling, 'He's gone, Roy, he's dead.'

Shaw dragged Adams up and then flattened him again with some powerful punches and threw in a couple of stomping kicks for good measure. On the tape, the knockdown was shown again in slow motion, as the piano chords of 'Jungleland' echoed gently. Roy cuddled and kissed his girl in the ring.

Next was an amateur evening at the Cat's Whiskers in Purley. There were thousands there, eating dinner before the show at long tables. Roy Shaw was at one, sipping drinks with jailhouse tattoos on his hand. He was introduced to the cheering crowds. Then Roy Shaw fought Paddy 'Mad Dog' Mullins before another packed house. There were more there than you'd see at a small-hall pro show, lots more. As Shaw climbed into the ring, Mullins was in his way, so he shoved him off. Shaw was a murderous puncher and he stalked Mullins from corner to corner before smashing him through the ropes.

The final bout matched Pretty Boy with Lenny McLean. As the crowd began to file in and take their seats, the camera focused on a trainer's bucket in the centre of the ring that was stuffed full of old green banknotes. A man in a suit was pulling out handfuls of them and counting them out on to the mat.

McLean was a huge man. His head was almost shaved, his nose crooked. He had vast, thick shoulders and a neck wider than his head. He was muscular but not defined. The real menace was not in his size but in his attitude. He was savage beyond any compromise, he was wild and he didn't know when to stop. To Lenny, a fight wasn't over when the other man went down. Roy Shaw seemed much smaller than McLean, but his own reputation was high. McLean ran at him immediately on the bell. It was like a cartoon fight. Lenny smashed Shaw's head from side to side, left, right, left, right. Only the punches kept Shaw up. Lenny stamped on him when he finally went down.

The tape fuzzed up and took a few seconds to settle back down. McLean, wearing a leather bomber jacket, walked into a pub looking like an extra from *The Sweeney*. Then he was in a ring. There was no indication of the name of his opponent. McLean was stripped to the waist and had on what looked like strongmen's tights and heavy boots. The other man panicked in fear when the two squared up to hear the referee's instructions, and in his panic he tried to get the first strike in. He attempted to headbutt McLean and brought his head quickly forwards, but not decisively enough. Lenny shook it off. He didn't bother waiting for the bell, he just rampaged in. He quickly knocked the man to the floor and he started jumping up and down on his head, smashing his foot down. Several men tried to pull him back and they did, but Lenny shook them off and landed a heavy kick on the fallen hero, who was still prone on the ring floor, deeply unconscious by the look of the way his arms flopped like a dead man's when McLean brought in the boot. There were plenty more fights on the tape, but those were for another time.

* * *

I went and saw the pub where Billy worked on the door. John said that he had worked there every night for twelve years despite his day job. Recently he'd cut back to just weekends because he was getting tired. The best doormen were paid around £60 a night. Billy received £85.

'That shows you what he's worth. He's a great deterrent. Nobody argues,' John explained. Billy's reputation had spread throughout London.

'I spent twelve months in Edgware with this girl,' John said one night when we sat outside in the courtyard of the Black Cap. 'And we went up to see this bloke at a pub in Cricklewood. And the gaffer says to me, "You don't come here often." Everyone was staring at me. He says, "Where do you come from?" I says, "Croydon." He says, "Oh, I had a hell of a lot of trouble with a bloke over there, at the Keys in Streatham. Billy. Do you know him?"

'I said, "No, I don't know him."

'"Oh, he's a bastard," he said. "He split my head with one punch." That was in north London. He's a legend.'

CHAPTER THREE

SCENES FROM THE LIFE
OF A HARD MAN

I'd known John for about three months when he came out with something astonishing.

'I've had three top-ten hits, you know.'

I looked at him, waiting for the punchline. But he was deadly serious.

'In the '60s it was, like. I was in a band called the Ivy League. "Tossing and Turning", that was the biggest song. Got to number two. I wrote that. I was called John Carter then. I was the singer. I split from them, and then they got another bloke in, and called him John Carter. There's about three Ivy Leagues doing the circuit now. Couple of blokes called John Carter. But I was the original one.'

Singing was the other strand of John's life, another part of him that had remained tucked away behind his ordinary days as a caretaker at a block of flats in Croydon. The two halves, singing and fighting, seemed so disparate that there could be nothing to link them to the same man, but John had an answer.

'Everything that's ever happened to me, the way I am, the fighting and the singing, all happened because of my stammer, like. It's not too bad now, talking to you, cos I feel relaxed, see? But when I'm under pressure, it can be real bad. I know what I want to say, but I can't get the words out. Any sort of formal situation, like a job interview, I can't handle it. They just think I'm a stuttering fool, like, and that gets me worked up, gets my temper up, like. So that's why I've never had a big job. It's why I started fighting, cos the other kids at school would take the piss out of me. Back when I was a kid, they didn't have all this speech therapy and stuff that I'd get now, so at school there were people who just thought I was an idiot. But singing can help you if you've got a really bad stammer, so that's how I found out that I could sing.'

From the stammer John came to boxing and to singing, and from there he began to carve out a direction for his life. Post-war Coventry, where he was born and brought up, was, John said, 'a shithole. I still hate the fucking place. People talk about rough towns, about tough inner cities, well, Coventry was a shit-hole then and it still is. A right small, shitty little city.'

The stammer ensured John a harsh childhood. There was something about his handicap and his natural size and his face that set him apart from the pack. His early schooldays left him with bitter memories, and it wasn't until he reached the age of eleven and walked into a gym for the first time that he found something that could mark him out.

'I trained and trained, right from when I was eleven. I started having fights as an amateur, back when being an amateur really meant something. Once I fought five times in a day. I was a decent amateur.'

Jack Bodell was a local hero and hard man, and later so was Danny McAlinden. John began to make a few waves locally, in the ring and on the streets. People who picked on his stammer lived to regret the experience.

'I've got huge stamina. Don't know where it comes from. I'm a counter-puncher. I let them come and do their bit, and then counter. I smoke, but my lungs are big, cos I've trained and trained since I was eleven years old.'

Aside from his natural attributes of size and bullish strength, John learned ringcraft. He had a theory about people who were born to fight. He always said that Billy Heaney, his Irish terror, was, and so were the greats like Duran and Hagler. He never mentioned his own name, but I was sure he would regard himself in that way. He had a natural cunning, something that could not be taught. He was a great defensive fighter. To fight in that way took great courage, courage to allow an opponent to come to you and lay his best shots on you while you trusted your skills to blunt and then overcome him.

John ran into some trouble in Coventry. He said that a local hard man suspected him of carrying on with his wife. He was ostracised by gangs of people. As his amateur career was coming to a head, he fought down in London, contested the ABAs and faced some of the big names of the day, including Pollen, the London policeman. At the same time, he was drawn to the '60s scene in the capital, and wanted to see if he could make it as a singer.

*   *   *

I looked up the Ivy League in the *Guinness Book of Hit Singles*. There they were, and there was 'Tossing and Turning' at number two in the charts, written by John Carter.

'We did all right. Played a lot of shows, did a lot of tours, like,' John explained. 'I wrote quite a lot of the songs. We were in with the bands of the day, John Mayall and that lot. I wanted to do more soul stuff, like, and they got another singer in and called him John Carter. I went to work with Paul Butterworth, who was a mate of mine from Coventry.'

'Tossing and Turning' still got played on the radio, and it had featured on lots of '60s retrospective albums, and in a recent edition of the music magazine *Mojo* they reviewed a reissue of some Ivy League material. The reviewer called John 'a respected vocalist'. I showed the review to him and wondered what it was worth.

'Nah. We were ripped off, like everyone was back then. I don't get anything. I know who the bloke is that owns them. I think he lives in Spain, like, or somewhere like that. We signed the rights away. It's so fucking complicated, like, what's happened to them, that I don't want anything to do with it. Someone's made a fucking lot of money, like, but it ain't me. Nah, I just want to get some good write-ups, do lots of shows . . .'

John's time in music prevented him from turning pro as a fighter, but he stayed in shape and held a trainer's licence with the British Boxing Board of Control. At the same time, he began to fight unlicensed, taking on anyone: doormen, bikers, bar-room heroes. More than thirty had stood before him down the years.

'I fought that Pretty Boy once,' John said, referring to the hard-eyed man who was on the videotape that Mickey had lent me. 'Roy Shaw. Place called the Cat's Whiskers. Jesus, he was a fucker. I just got hold of him and didn't let go. Wrestled him.'

John didn't punch out Shaw, but he took out nearly everyone else, using his usual tactic of waiting for the whirlwind to blow out before hammering away at their senses.

* * *

John came to Croydon when he was still young and raw. He was already hardened to people's reaction to him. He was an outsider. When you got past his stammer, his accent marked him out still further. He was big and noticeable. He knew that the way to survive was to give little of himself away, so he kept hidden behind a façade of aggression. He got a job driving a mini-cab. His first night showed him what Croydon was all about.

'This controller, right, fucking didn't like me. He gave me this fare, and said the bloke would be waiting for me at this house. I wrote down the address and everything.'

John drove to the house. It was a big place and it looked empty. No one came out of the house when he sounded his horn. He went and knocked on the door. No answer. He went around the back: still no answer, and no one waiting. John checked the address again. He looked through the windows, and knocked on both doors again. There was no sign of his fare. The controller came over the radio.

'Have you picked up the fare yet?'

'No, he ain't here,' John replied.

'You're at the wrong fucking place, then.'

'I ain't,' John told him.

'Check the address.'

'I . . . I . . . just did.'

'Well, he's just phoned, and you ain't there.'

'I am, I'm telling you.'

John went back to the house and knocked again, looking around for any sign he could find that would help him.

Back in the car, the radio went again.

'Have you picked up yet?'

'He . . . He . . . He . . .' The stress was affecting John's stammer.

'Look, you fucking stuttering idiot, fucking get it sorted.'

That did it for John. He returned to his car and drove back to the cab firm's office.

'I found the fucking controller and I said, "Don't you ever fucking talk to me like that, you cunt," and I chucked his fucking radio back at him and fucking did him, like. Smashed the place up a bit and walked out.'

* * *

After his brutal introduction to life in Croydon, John began to find his feet. There were a couple of pubs side by side and he got work at one as a doorman. Soon he was matey with most of the men there and his horizons began to expand. Life was less bleak. He went through a couple of gang wars on the doors, where his huge presence and his naturally cool nature saw everyone through. He first found Danny's gym way back before it was called Danny's, when it was run by an old guy named Eddie.

'He was a funny old bloke. He had a stick, like,' John remembered, 'and he'd sit on this little stool in the corner, and when the sparring got out of hand he'd bang his stick on the ground and scream at you to stop.'

One evening John walked in and there was Billy Heaney. John didn't take too much notice until he saw Billy get into the ring for a move around. Billy was a young man then, and all the power I'd seen up close was allied to a more athletic frame and a more youthful vigour. After a while he asked John for a spar, and John got in for the first of hundreds of rounds.

'It was fucking mad, like, that first time. He whacked me with some big shots, real hard. I wasn't going to take it, and it was like a war in there. Old Eddie was jumping up and down, banging his stick on the floor. He was yelling "Break it up, break it up" at the top of his voice. Nearly bust his fucking stick . . .'

The savage exchanges forged a lasting bond between the older fighter and the younger man. Billy, so quiet, and John, sometimes the opposite, worked off each other in the time-honoured way. The ring sharpened their friendship and yet never tempered their aggression. Billy knocked John out four or five times, but he took the knockdowns as trophies.

'When he hit me, it was like a numbness. Your senses just go.' John was describing the vague area of the brain that Muhammad Ali called 'the near room'. I told him about Ali's description of being tagged by George Foreman: 'Take a stiff tree branch in your hand and hit it against the floor and you'll feel your hand go "boingggg". Well, getting hit is the same kind

51

of jar on your whole body, and you need at least ten or twelve seconds to make that go away. You get hit again before that, you get another "boingggg".'

'That's exactly it,' John agreed. 'He smacks you on the nose and you think he's caught you on the forehead because your system's in shock from the punch, like.'

John began to work Billy hard and launched him into the unlicensed game – albeit with some small regrets. He felt that Billy would have made an excellent pro if he had taken charge of him when he was younger.

Instead, their friendship led them in other directions. John began to visit the pub where Billy worked on the door. It was an Irish joint, a wild place kept in order only by Billy's mighty hitting power and his alliance with Dave the Landlord, another toughie from across the Irish Sea, and a giant of a man known only as Hoxton Tom. The three operated as a kind of volunteer trouble-shooting squad, appearing like uncaped crusaders at other establishments which were facing trouble.

'They were fucking hard,' John said. 'You'd fucking call them in if you had bother. I remember once, I went out to meet Billy and I got to the pub and the bloke there said, "Oh, they're not here. There's trouble over at the Queen's. Load of bikers have taken it over."

'So I went down there quick as I could, and I walked in the car park, and it was like a scene from one of those fucking *Rambo* films. There were bikes knocked all over the car park, smashed up. Loads of unconscious bikers on the floor and a load of others getting away as fast as they could. The three of them, Billy, Dave and Hoxton Tom, they'd gone in there with baseball bats, like, and sorted the lot of them out.

'Another time, there was this bloke giving Billy some shit on the door. No one usually argues with him, because he's a legend, right? But Billy had barred this geezer and he was determined to come in. So he goes over the road and takes a fucking run up at the door. He's charging at it, like. And he gets as far as Billy, and Billy just fucking backhands him.' John demonstrated, wafting out his large paw. 'Didn't even punch him, just CRACK! with the back of his hand. They had to carry the bloke off.'

John brought me a video tape of some of his early sparring sessions with Billy, so I could get an idea of the kind of fighter he had been. Both of the sessions were at Danny's. At first I didn't recognise Billy. He looked so much younger, with a big mop of blond curls. But there was no mistaking his style: head low, the curiously high leading step forwards, the hissing arcs of his shots. John's bulky manoeuvring was instantly recognisable too. I saw again what a skilful fighter he was. He moved his body with a minimum of effort, but he was almost like a Zen Master, making infinitesimal adjustments to alter the flow, the mood.

Television lends an unreal shimmer to boxing. It robs it of its inherent bloodiness, its gasps of pain, its pitiless agonies and little deaths. There is none of the spraying sweat, the squeals and squalls of approaching defeat and impending doom. But with the visceral elements removed, the tape allowed me to see another side of the pair. Robbed of his power, if only by the distance of the video tape, Billy was a cumbersome man. His virtues in the flesh were camouflaged by the screen. But John's were enhanced. What looked like a series of unrelated and hasty manoeuvres when seen up close actually seemed to make more sense. John would slip a shot and then return. He could defend a long attack and not take a single punch on a vulnerable spot; he could smother and swarm and frustrate, and then he was ready to move in and land his own stiff shots. The tape jolted again. Now Billy was in with a big lad whom John had picked out as a bit of a troublemaker at the gym. He was always a mouthy character, talking himself up and putting everyone else down. He talked like a champ, talked like a Tyson, but Billy soon sucked the juice from his boasts. They moved for a few rounds, and Billy gained ground in each one. Then some jarring shots and it was over. The bigger man backed down.

John's words came back to me: 'If I'd had him when he was twenty-one, I'd've put him in with any heavyweight in the country . . .'

* * *

A big-money offer came in for John. He was asked if he wanted to travel to Seattle to fight a biker from Detroit, a wild man with a big reputation. There were thousands on the table. John considered the offer for a long time.

'Trouble with America is, there's legends walking around on the street. There's so much talent. You don't know who you might be fighting. If it's an ex-pro you could be in trouble. We heard he was a biker, a bit of a Hell's Angel, like. When they said that, we said, "Yeah, we'll fight him." If he'd said he was a boxer, we'd have said no.'

The biker's backers offered John a return ticket to Seattle and a ticket for someone to act as a second, plus the prize money and a night in a hotel. John took a man well known in boxing circles. He didn't want to tell me who it was, but he said that I would be aware of who he was.

They arrived at the hotel in Seattle. John was keen to get a look at the man he'd be stepping through the ropes with. He was out of luck. The first time they would come face to face would be at the fight.

John and his second passed some uneasy hours as the bout approached. It was held out on the fringes of the city. The place was packed with bikers, and there was a car park full of long-forked machines. John's nerves calmed a little. The guy really was going to be a biker. Inside, he was approached by the promoters and told that the fight should go for the full four rounds. It was dressed up to sound like a warning to John not to lie down or take a dive, but he hadn't come six thousand miles to fall over. No, he understood the undertone of the discussion. If he got on top he was to carry his man through to the final bell, not knock him senseless.

John warmed himself up and gloved up. The usual brew of fear and dread and adrenaline knotted up his guts. Just like he always said, 'The walk to the ring, when you're cold – that's the hardest thing you'll ever do.'

He faced that walk now, taking those long, cold yards step by step as he shrugged his big shoulders to free them of the acid tensions of the moment. He heard little of the crowd around him. Here, in the desolate wastelands of the mind, was where most fights were won and lost. Bravado counted for nothing in this unknown and distant arena.

It was hard to imagine, after all the hardships of his life, that these moments were the worst for John, that this transitory journey was so full of pain and horror.

'It's the hardest thing you'll ever do . . .'

He stepped into the ring. The walk was over. He eyed his opponent, and what he saw pleased him.

'He was just big and fat. Bloody bar-room hero. It wasn't going to be that much of a problem.'

The scrap began. The biker grabbed John and tried to wrestle him to the ground. That was too hard a job for him. John pushed him back. With some canvas between them, the biker ducked down and threw his head up, looking for the butt. John moved away again and landed with clean punches. The biker grabbed hold of him again, instigating a dark dance to the corner. He threw a leg out, trying to kick the legs from under John.

'I didn't let him get that far, I just hammered and hammered and hammered. Kept him off me. It went the four rounds.'

The win was unequivocal. Not even the most biased hometowner could have denied John the result. He was handed a five-figure sum in cash, in a zip-up bag. John and his second returned to their hotel, but they couldn't sleep. They expected the bikers to come back for the money.

'We had the money in our hotel, and we thought that they were gonna kick the door in and take it off us, so we got a cab to the airport and stayed there. It was a lot of money. In the thousands. In pounds. I heard from the bloke that I had the fight with a couple of times afterwards, and I saw him once in a film. It had Charles Bronson in it, and all these bikers. He was an extra. If it's bikers, we'll say, yeah, we'll fight a biker, cos you're in no danger at all . . .'

*   *   *

The summer came slipping along. The Black Cap had a court-yard at the rear of its long back bar. After training John would take his Guinness and blackcurrant and slide his nineteen-stone frame gingerly on to one of the thin benches that were attached to the wooden tables, and we would sit through the warm nights, shooting the breeze as the last of the sun dipped below the high-rises of south London.

'Did I tell you about Joe Frazier?' he asked, looking up over the lip of his pint.

'Christ, John, you never fought him, did you?'

'Fucking nearly did,' he replied, setting his glass down.

'What?' I'd heard a few of the big man's wilder tales, but Smokin' Joe himself . . .

'He had a band, see. The Knockouts, they were called, like a big sort of soul review thing. After he fought Ali for the third time, I think it was about '75 this happened, he brought this band over here for a tour. He was on TV with it. I was the warm-up man, like, the opening act. At first he fucking hated me. First couple of weeks of the tour, he never really said a word to me at all. We were going round all these halls, and he was a real hard worker. He could have just turned up and done a couple of numbers, like, but he did a pretty decent show with an interval and stuff. He wasn't a bad singer at all, really. For a boxer, anyhow . . .' John looked up, his little half-smile playing at the corners of his mouth.

'Anyway, then he finds out I'm a fighter, right? And I can't fucking get away from him. He won't leave me alone. I think he was getting a bit bored, like, with all the travelling, and he was a boxer, he liked boxing people. So I'm riding round in the limo with him everywhere, and we're having a real good laugh. Jesus, he was a strong bastard. Only little he was, but really fucking muscley and solid. Big, strong neck, like.' John made a circle around his own bull-neck with his hands to emphasise the point. I laughed. Only a man of John's bulk could describe Joe Frazier as 'little'.

'In the car, he'd grab hold of me, and I could feel his strength, like. He was like an ox. He'd grab hold of me and I'd really fucking feel it, you know.

'So he says to me, "C'mon, John, you and me, we'll find a gym and have a spar." I thought, "Jesus Christ, I don't fucking fancy that much."

'I says to him, "Joe, I ain't gonna do it, mate. You're too small. I'll kill you. I don't wanna hurt you . . ." Course, this makes him mad. He's fucking knocked lumps out of Muhammad Ali, like. KO'd Earnie Shavers. He got a bit wound up, Joe did. Had a bit of a short fuse, he did. He'd blow his top at me. Every day, he'd say, "C'mon, John, let's find a gym. Just you and me in the ring." And every day I'm like, "Joe, I ain't doing it. I'll kill you. I'm too big for you."

'But really, every time we get into a place and he's trying to find a gym, I'm thinking, "Please, God, don't let him find one." I kept trying to distract him, like. Anyway, night after night, he's looking to get us in the ring, and I manage to get out of it, right until the very last night of the tour. Cardiff, I think it was, somewhere like that. Joe comes rushing up and he goes, "Done it, John. There's a place just up the road. We can go there. We've got some kit. Come on."

'"Oh Christ," I think to myself. I go down there, and I can't get out of it. I'm thinking about all the times I've told him I'd do him, like. And he's laughing away, bouncing round the ring. In I go, and he sticks his jab out, and it was like "bang". It was only a jab, but he was a strong feller. I felt it. So I doubled up, like this.' John stood up, clutching his belly, pretending he was winded.

'Frazier comes running over. "You all right, John? You all right?" And I got back up and I went 'WHACK' and popped him one in the stomach. Then I just jumped out of the ropes as fast as I could. He was chasing me all round the gym, going, "Come back, you motherfucker, come back." We had a right laugh about it, as well.

'We tricked him again, too. Told him that there was this other bloke after him at some nightclub. Joe was going, "Show me where he is, then." We'd go, "He was over there a minute ago, Joe. Says he's going to kill you." He'd be jumping around looking for the guy. Eyes bulging, like. He was easy to wind up. Lovely feller, though, he was. He used to send me a card every Christmas. Never forgot.'

* * *

John had once trained a young prospect at Danny's. The kid was a good, hard fighter, quick and neat in the way that young boxers can be. John would get into the ring with him and urge the kid to him, taking combinations on his broad arms and administering a canny slap or two through the blur of youthful effort. John would hand down master classes in pain to build endurance and courage in his man. As the months rolled by, he inducted the boy into the ways of the squared circle. The prospect was ill-disciplined outside the ring, but in his boxing he was the opposite. He responded to the spartan rituals of the game, and he built his strength through denial. He was fit and cocky. He played the field and he began an affair with a married woman. Inevitably, the woman's husband got to hear about his wife's infidelity, and then he found out the identity of her lover.

John and the young fighter stepped on to the pavement outside Danny's after training, and John saw that a car was parked awkwardly on the other side of the road. The prospect was walking on the side of the pavement nearest the car. In the time it took John to look up and notice that the car was in a strange place, a shotgun poked through the open window.

'I saw it and I grabbed hold of the kid, like, tried to spin him round. But then "BLAAAM" . . .' John motioned a rifle being fired.

The bullet went through the kid's back and severed his spinal cord. John held him in his arms on the rough kerbside until the ambulance came.

'It's sad, really. The silly fucker still thinks he's going to fight again,' John said. 'But he ain't . . .'

* * *

There was one more video tape for me to watch. It was another fight at Danny's gym, an unlicensed bout for an invited audience, who sat in neat rows of chairs in front of that familiar, scruffy ring. The fighters were both women. One was a friend of John's, a girl named Sally, a tall, attractive blonde with fine cheekbones and a generous mouth set in a slim face. It didn't look like a face that could take a punch, yet she trained down at Danny's quite often and was respected by every man in the place. She was fit and strong. John had prepared her for this fight, and he had been impressed by her stamina and her skill. Sally loved the game, but at the time of the fight there were no avenues for female fighters other than the unlicensed one.

Sally's opponent was called Carol, and she had travelled up to London from the south coast. She was a good few inches shorter than Sally, with protruding front teeth and straggly, mousey hair that had been shaved at the sides and allowed to grow long at the back in a redneck cut.

'A good fighter,' John told me. 'She was a lesbian, like . . .' he added conspiratorially.

John stood at the centre of the ring. He was the referee, and he'd donned a white shirt and a bow tie for the occasion.

Both women wore vests and shorts and they fought out six two-minute rounds. Sally was by far the superior boxer and in each of the rounds from the second she pushed Carol to the corners and kept her pinned there with some sharp punches. Carol was tough, though. She stayed on her feet and shrugged off all the attempts John made to stop the fight. When the final bell went, everyone stood up and applauded. It had looked like a good amateur fight between competitors who had come to box, to show their skills. Whether it was once again the distance of the video tape or the unexpected calibre of the contest, I don't know, but it was in no way a disturbing thing. Although perhaps it should have been: two women scrapping for a few hundred pounds in front of an audience of men in a shabby gym under a decrepit pub in the backstreets of south London.

* * *

'I got a gig on, at the Arts Centre up near Beckenham. Come along.'

I'd been waiting for the chance to fit the final piece into the remarkable saga of John's ordinary, extraordinary life. His boxing credentials, which had seemed questionable way back when we first touched gloves, had all been borne out. I had no reason to doubt his showbiz standing, but it was hard to reconcile the indelible images of his dark bulk shifting around the loose ring at Danny's, his almost casual acquaintance with the spartan brutality of boxing, with the idea of him squeezing into a fancy shirt and belting out the hits of all our yesterdays.

'What will you be singing, all your old stuff?'

'Nah. Bit of soul, bit of Motown, like. Oldies but goodies, as they say,' he added, with his little half-smile.

Even Mickey had never seen John sing, but he'd 'heard that he was bloody good'.

John was appearing under the name of John Carter at the Arts Centre, which was a spruced-up old mansion on the road between Beckenham and Croydon. The gig was not in the main theatre but in a back bar, which was glass-fronted. There were about a hundred or so people inside, sitting around clusters of tables and drinking. John appeared, dressed all in black. He looked trimmer than he did in his gym gear, and he'd taken a certain swagger from the ring, too. His band were two guys with acoustic guitars, one an old hippy with the look of a low-rent Eric Clapton about him. They went on first to open up the show. It was dreadful. Bad. The guitars were buzzing and distorting through the little PA, and their voices had hard edges that stopped any sort of harmony in its tracks. They limped through the expected repertoire of Crowded House and 'the Stones' and 'one from the late, great John Lennon – join in if you like', plus assorted others, before inviting a woman up on stage for a shambolic version of a Tracy Chapman number. They had to stop in the middle and begin again.

'Fucking hell,' John muttered. After a while, he got up from our table and started fiddling with the knobs on the little mixing desk. I told him the best thing he could do was turn it right down, and his usual good humour almost deserted him. I suddenly realised how bad I'd feel for him if he really couldn't sing. I took some heart from the review in the music magazine that had described him as 'respected'. I hoped they'd got the right John Carter.

So then, after a slightly gloomy interval during which he said he was 'going to have to sort the band out', John went on. He didn't bother standing up on the small stage; instead, he grabbed the microphone from its stand and took the floor just in front of the first row of tables. The band started up, strumming out the intro to the old Animals number '(Oh Please) Don't Let Me Be Misunderstood'. It was almost like the start of a fight. There was no going back now. There would be an unequivocal outcome.

John began: '*Baby, it's been so hard for me . . .*'

I rocked back in my hard chair. His voice was good. Not just good but great, a big, black soulful voice that came out somewhere between Joe Cocker and Andrew Strong, the fat kid who sang the songs in *The Commitments*. Somehow, John's voice was full enough to fill the gaps between the guitars that his band had lacked the ability to do. He gelled everything together with a great big grin before roaring out the 'I'm just a boy whose intentions are good' line. Relief was my overriding emotion. Just as his strange life had been hidden away, so had this voice. Once again it seemed that his days could have easily followed a different path, such was the authentic quality of his singing. The Big Fella was the real thing. People whooped along with the songs. John wasn't going to be ripping up any charts, but he was carrying everyone along. He was best on the slow numbers, making 'Ain't No Sunshine When She's Gone' sound almost like the authentic Bill Withers version, and then taking a slow, slow cover of 'Rainy Night in Georgia' way downbeat.

Afterwards, he pulled hard on his pint of Guinness and blackcurrant and nodded over at a middle-aged lady who kept staring at him.

'See her,' he said, in a sly whisper. 'She's my number one fan. Goes everywhere I've got a gig, like. Fancies me like mad. I have to fight her off, like . . .'

John grinned wolfishly, but soon he was forced into a long conversation with her, from which he kept looking up and rolling his eyes about. He raised his glass and sank the remains of his drink, soothing the chords that could leave him stammering 'like a fool' and singing like a broken-down angel.

CHAPTER FOUR

NO PRICE TAG ON THEIR HONOUR

The sound of Billy on the heavy bag permeated Danny's gym. He would start like this: tap . . . tap . . . with his left fist. He was just pushing his arm away from his body, but the bag would still begin to swing and the top links of the chain that held it to the ceiling would start to grate against each other and squeak. Then he'd pop a right into the battered black leather. It didn't look like a hard shot, but this time the bag would jump a little on its chain. Once Billy got the heavy bag swinging he'd begin to pound: left, left . . . and then right . . . WHACK; left, left . . . right . . . WHACK; left, left . . . right . . . WHACK. Air wheezed out of the bag with every slap. The noise from the chain punctuated Billy's swings.

John Barnwell would look on, his pleasure tempered by the knowledge that those same shots would soon be beating out a rhythm on his ribcage. We'd stand together and watch as the bag swung.

'The little bastard doesn't know his strength sometimes,' said John. 'If you're in with him having a move around, like, he'll get a bit carried away. Let a few go.'

Every time I visited the gym, Billy looked fitter. His face was always ruddy from the outdoor work, and now his cheekbones were starting to poke through and his gut was disappearing. He could blow up to nineteen, even twenty stone when he was not training, but when Billy was fit his optimum weight was around seventeen and a half stone. He always trained in a T-shirt, old jogging pants and ancient trainers which he never laced up. Like Tyson, he wore no socks. Before, he had appeared huge but shapeless – no neck, beefy shoulders, big arms and the rest an amorphous mass – but now he was becoming honed. There was nothing in particular you could point to, he was just getting sharper, tighter. His bulk was closing in on itself, huddling on his frame. He was compact and wound up. He was getting ready.

He and John slipped between the ropes and stood in opposing corners, waiting for the old clock's timer to tick around to mark the start of three minutes. They'd both strapped on headguards. The buzzer sounded and both moved to the centre of the ring. Billy was leaden-footed as he edged forwards and his head dipped down as he snorted and expelled breath heavily. He cuffed John around, but John was wily. He covered up, tucked in his chin and protected his sides. When Billy got too close he'd wrap a huge paw around his neck and wrestle him in, where he'd whack him in the sides. Billy seemed unbothered. After two rounds he'd slowed John down a little and his body shots landed with echoing thumps. John would shift his sides around laterally for some relief, but Billy was relentless. He could only fight in one way, by moving forwards and hitting at full power.

John shook his head after three rounds and pulled off his headguard. Billy came over and gave him a friendly tap. Someone else stepped in for a spar and John retreated to the little old ringside bench to watch.

'Fucker hurt me round the ribs,' he winced. John paused for a few moments, and his big face began to regain its usual pallor. He grinned his little mouth-turned-up-at-the-edges grin.

'He broke one of my ribs once, you know. It was agony. I couldn't catch my breath. He drove me down to casualty, and the nurses put me on a trolley, and I couldn't even tell them what was wrong. So I'm lying there, and they've pulled my top off and attached these things to my fingers, and then this nurse comes in and starts shaving my chest. Because I was sweating so hard cos I'd been sparring, they thought I was having a heart attack. Billy's there in the corner of the room, like, just looking guilty, and I'm saying to them, "I've . . . broken . . . my . . . fucking . . . ribs," one word at a time because I can't get any air in.'

After the sparring was finished, I stood up and walked over to Billy, who was standing in the corner, holding a squash bottle between his gloves and tilting it all over his face. Dribbles of water spilled into his mouth. Steam came off him, and he smelt like a wet dog. He raised his eyebrows in acknowledgement.

'You looked good tonight,' I said.

'Yeah, yeah.' His voice came in little gasps, accompanied by twitches of his head. He seemed nervous, barely able to talk.

'You enjoying it, then?'

'Oh, I love it,' he lilted in his soft brogue. 'I love it . . .'

I smiled, and he lifted his head up a little, a twinkle in his soft eyes.

'I love it,' he said again.

* * *

Beyond that admission, it was hard to draw any more out of Billy. The reasons behind his passion for fighting remained his own. John and Mickey and anyone who had stepped into the ring shared at least part of the secret, and he had allowed John to tell me a little about his life, but the part that I wanted to know about the most was the part he probably couldn't even begin to describe beyond those three words: 'I love it.'

One night I got to the gym and there was no one there except for one white boy, who was banging away on a bag, and his trainer, an old man of the kind you only ever seem to find sitting around in boxing gyms.

The fighter stood waiting for the ring-clock on the wall to finish its minute's break before it counted down another three. He was a cheery boxer, a middleweight who was going slightly to seed. His stomach was bulging against his grey aertex T-shirt. Sweat dampened his close-cropped hair and ran down his nose, which had been squashed at the bottom. It also seemed to have buckled in the middle, giving him an almost Roman look.

The buzzer on the ring-clock sounded and he went about his work. He had a big right hand, which he loved to wind up and thud into the bag. It was an impressive shot for a small man, even if he was a slow mover, heavy on his feet.

He stopped when the three minutes were up.

'You looked miles away then,' his trainer told him.

'Yeah,' the fighter said, his face lighting up. 'I'm always like that, I drift off. Could be anywhere then, couldn't I? Vegas, Atlantic City, Detroit, New York . . .'

Maybe those were the feelings Billy enjoyed too, in his mind turning an empty, rundown gym by a shabby south London pub into one of the great Meccas of boxing, throwing his shots with the best of them, letting some good guys feel his weight. Maybe that was a part of the love.

*   *   *

The man that Billy was getting ready for was an unlicensed heavyweight 'champion' who went by the ring name of Steve The Hammer. Steve The Hammer had just come out of prison for an unspecified crime of violence and he was back on the streets of his childhood. He was rebuilding his life in his own unconventional way, picking up the threads of his early career as a doorman and as a streetfighter. Steve was a big man, solidly built with a typical white heavyweight's physique: broad shoulders and a big chest and arms, but without anything much in the way of muscle definition. He had kept himself in shape on the inside. Now he was out and he was training hard. Before he went to prison, Steve had whacked out a lot of men in the unlicensed game, and he had a good following. He had been, in the local parlance, a 'face' – meaning that he was known as a tough fighter, a man to be respected.

In many ways Steve had the classic unlicensed fighter's

profile, right down to the nickname. He had a background of violence that had been channelled by some early training in the gym as a young teen. He was a reasonably promising amateur fighter who felt the pull of the streets a little too hard. Instead of remaining dedicated and keeping out of trouble, he fell in with the wrong people. His criminal record began to stretch out from petty crime to bigger set pieces. He stayed sharp by going training, and someone at a gym somewhere had made him a match. His style was perfect for the unlicensed game. He was a fearless fighter, an attribute that served him well as a doorman, and he loved to come forward throwing punches. He could hit, too, another legacy of the door, and he was no coward. It all added up to a decent package, and he had become a crowd-pleaser who could shift plenty of tickets for his fights. His following extended over north-east London.

Steve The Hammer was the flip side of the anti-boxing debate. The sport could have kept him on the straight and narrow, but instead the lure of the city's streets and life in the demi-monde drew him in. His natural toughness and aggression dictated his course. Now he was about to meet another man who had many of the same qualities.

The match had been made by way of a challenge to Billy by a well-known south London promoter called Trevor Foster. Trev owned a gym, but it was frequented by bodybuilders rather than boxers. Many huge men trained there, chewing steroids as they went. Trev himself was a squat powerhouse who could bench-press giant poundages. He had a reputation as a top promoter. His matches were well made through a series of contacts like John, and his bills usually provided good value for the ticket-buyers. He also had access to some good venues, nightclubs that were happy to turn themselves over for the night in return for a good take at the bar. He had once helped John to put his own show together, and John seemed to regard him with a degree of affection, even if it was tempered with a healthy scepticism.

Trev and John thought that the match between Billy and Steve could be considered an unofficial championship. Neither of them knew of any better heavyweight sluggers currently active in the area.

Billy trained hard for the fight. John showed me another tape of him sparring at the gym. He was in the ring with Kev, a regular at Danny's then, who achieved cult status by going in with Billy and goading him. They sparred four or five cagey rounds and then Kev unloaded, stinging Billy. Billy looped a big overhand right and Kev's head dropped forward on to Billy's shoulders – and when he lifted it up again you could see he'd left a spreading slick of dark red blood across Billy's sweat-soaked T-shirt. His nose had been pulped across the middle of his face. He lifted a glove up and it came away covered in snot and gore, so he smiled and shook his head, and the session ended.

John's method of training was quite unique too. Like many trainers, he had the harsh wisdom of thousands of rounds. What he also had was nineteen stone of bulk and a lithe boxing brain that allowed him to get in between the ropes with his men and give them some instruction from the sharp end. It was an uncomfortable method, but it gave John a good perspective on his man. He could feel for himself the improvement in his fighters, and he could hand out some painful reminders of their mistakes. John was a good fighter to watch. He seemed to shuffle around, but his movements were precise. He was always going somewhere, with some purpose: to weaken the effects of an opponent's attacks, or to change their world view, or to better deliver some medicine of his own.

John was happy with Billy's form, and he was pleased and excited by the prospects of the fight with Steve, but he also had plenty of gnawing doubts. The fight was fixed in a club on the other side of London, for a start. He knew that he and Billy would be heavily outnumbered. It even crossed his mind that they may have to 'do a runner' should things go the wrong way. As the match grew closer, so John's fears grew. Billy seemed to be less concerned. He'd sold out his allocation of tickets, so he'd have the benefit of a few of his supporters there at least. And to Billy, backing away from the prospect of a fight was an alien concept. It wasn't anything that would occur to him.

* * *

The day of the fight came soon enough. John woke up feeling edgy and nervous, and he couldn't quite figure out why. His unease had nothing to do with Billy's capabilities in the ring, but with the odds that had been loaded so heavily against him by Trev's promotion. Pro fighters might fly thousands of miles from home to take on a champion, but he and Billy were travelling as far as any had ever done, just by crossing London. The fight was on foreign turf, on hostile territory, across the barricades. John woke up and wondered not if Billy would fight well enough, but if he himself might have to slug it out, just to get away with their money or with their heads intact. The day dragged. John spoke to Billy, who was quiet, as quiet as he'd ever been.

They made an arrangement to meet with Mickey and a few other boys, when they'd take a van across town to the fight.

At least John had something up front, from the few tickets he'd had for Billy. Trev told him that the fight would be packed. Steve The Hammer was a popular man.

John's truest belief about Billy, formed over the hours in and out of the ring with him, made during the scraps and the scrapes and fighting and fucking about, was that he was born to fight. 'Some people just are,' he told me. 'Roberto Duran, he was. Tyson is. So is Billy, y'know.'

But under extreme pressure was where true character came out. Billy was so quiet, he seemed coiled up. When he unwound, who knew? He was like a Tyson, in many strange little ways. He was a similar build, and he had the same soft, almost girlish voice but without the lisp. And he had the same history of streetfighting, of disputes settled and territory held, of internal, self-defined codes of honour adhered to. Billy had never backed off or backed down. He was a progeny of violence, a dark star that came as rarely as a comet, a man who flourished in the pain and who revelled in being hit and withstanding it. He grew mightier in his suffering. No, there was no doubt that Billy would fight. The doubt came about when – or even whether – he would stop. The sense that they were here in the margins, on the very edges of sport, came across strongly. The boundaries could be pushed so far back that they no longer mattered. Everything could be permitted. The day began to close around them like a fist.

The van moved around south-east London, filling up with its motley crew. John began to brief Billy about the night ahead. They would arrive at the venue after the other fights had begun. John was very anxious to limit their time there. Years of experience had taught him every trick and every stroke, and he was wary.

The problems with a fight like this were many. The promotion was out of John's hands. He had to deliver his part of the bargain – Billy – up front, and then collect afterwards. He had no idea how difficult that would be, how much muscle would be stacked against him. He was partly terrified that Billy would win, especially convincingly. Then things really could turn nasty. After so many years, John had a nose for situations like this, and this one was definitely making his nose twitch. His stammer and his nervous tics had returned.

The van edged along. Everyone sat quietly. The contents of Billy's mind would forever remain his and his alone. For John, every stop at an amber light, every bumper-to-bumper encounter, was a miniature jail sentence. The waiting was always the worst part.

* * *

There was a light rain falling, and the last of the daylight had given way to the artificial neons of the grubby streets: the tired fast-food outlets with their less-than-household names that were found in the more neglected parts of the city, such as Chicken King and Starburger; the green and purple lights of the Indian restaurants; the red and white of a bingo hall. The streets around here sagged with the efforts of survival. People scurried along them with little purpose other than to keep out of the rain.

The venue for the fight was a nightclub that was called

something grandiose like Caesar's Palace or Aladdin's, some silly, self-aggrandising Vegas notion. There was no more glamour to it than there was to the shops nearby, or the dark alley that led around the back. The van nosed its way down there.

John told the others to wait in the van while he undertook an initial recce. He nudged open a fire door, the bar and ratchet making a racket dragging on the concrete, and took the back stairs towards the office area. He found one room occupied by Steve The Hammer and his men. The Hammer was jumping around and loosening up. John said nothing. He located Trev, whom he found in an upbeat mood.

'Fucking hell, it looks good, John,' he told him. 'There's a fucking lot of people here. It's a big night. How's your boy?'

'He's here, mate. That's all you need to know, like,' John replied, and grinned. 'I see that Steve The Hammer's here too, then. Billy better get a fucking room like he's got, mate.'

'I've got him somewhere,' Trev claimed.

John looked at Trev. Trev was a short man, but he was heavily muscled. He had beaten many men like that in his own fighting career. Big muscles had nothing to do with it. Look at Frank Bruno.

Trev knew everyone there. He was tight with Steve The Hammer's crew. John wanted to tie him down about the money from the fight.

'You'll get it after,' Trev told him. 'Come and meet me back at the gym. I'm not going to carry it round here.'

That seemed wise enough to John. There were plenty of men about who wouldn't need asking twice if they got a sniff of a bag full of notes.

'Come on your own, though,' Trev told him.

John said nothing. He knew better than to disagree at this point.

'Bring him in when you're ready,' Trev said, and was gone.

John walked into the nightclub. There had been a few bouts on the card already. The ring was in the middle of what was usually the dance floor. Maybe six hundred people were milling around. Some were standing about the ring, but most of them were down at the bar. Men lined up four or five deep for beer. There was money changing hands, betting money. John stood about, trying to pick up a vibe. There were very few faces he recognised, and he realised that nearly everyone in the place was a follower of Steve The Hammer.

'I started to think, "Fuck, we'll have to get out of here sharpish after,"' he said later. 'I thought that there could easily be a fucking riot here, especially if Billy won. We might have to do a runner.'

He returned to the van and brought everyone in. He led Billy up the back stairs and into one of the little office rooms.

Billy dropped his kit-bag and began to prepare. He would fight bare-chested. He wore a pair of decent boxing boots and tracksuit trousers. John bandaged his hands up, winding the material carefully around Billy's raised knuckles. Soon his fists looked like they were recovering from a long surgical procedure. John pulled some brown fourteen-and-a-half-ounce gloves over the bandages and tied them off. Then he taped over the rough laces.

Billy had been sitting with his head bowed, but now he jumped up and started to get a sweat on. His gut still protruded a little, but plenty of heavyweights were at their best with a layer of fat under the skin. It gave them bulk and reserves of stamina. Billy's body was far from ripped, but he was carrying huge slabs of muscle deep on his frame. His shoulders were vast and square, his neck a thick rope of tendon and sinew. His mouth was narrow.

'Look, we might have to fucking get out quick after. Be ready.'

Billy nodded. John was to be in Billy's corner. He said he would jump through the ropes at the end and grab Billy's arm and they'd make their way out from there.

Trev came and gave them the nod. They began the long walk to the ring and I remembered John's words the first time we ever spoke about boxing, licensed or otherwise: 'Everybody thinks it's easy to fight. They go into a pub and fight three or four blokes, knock them down. But the average pub fight lasts eighteen seconds. When you get in the ring, it's more controlled. In the dressing-room, you're thinking, "I've got to fight this bloke." And you're cold. You're not mad at him. All your nerves are going, your stomach's going, your body is playing terrible tricks on you. All your mates are going "C'MON" . . .'

When Billy and John entered the club, there was a roar. The bar had emptied and there were tight and serried ranks of fight fans around the ring. Up in the balcony there were more. The house lights had gone down and just the lights above the dance floor were on. They were a strange mixture, with several different coloured gels on them. They were moody rather than bright, and they added further to the menace of the occasion. The atmosphere was edging towards something ferocious. This was a room full of rough men who had paid good money to see a fight. The fighters would be expected to give everything now. The men were not here to see pussy tactics, exhibitions of skill or a spoiling game. They were here to see two hard men test themselves against each other. They were here to see that violence was carried out and seen to be carried out. I could only guess what was in Billy's head as he made his way through them. He stood in the ring and looked around briefly.

Then came The Hammer, to cheers and shouts of encouragement.

'C'mon, Stevey . . .'

'C'mon, Stevey boy . . .'

'Let's have the fucking paddy, Steve . . .'

He made it to the ring. He was taller than Billy, but nowhere near as solid. His hair had been razored lower, and he looked like what he was, a streetfighter. He was unable to keep himself still. His eyes were narrow. It went through John Barnwell's head that maybe he was on speed. No, but he looked keen and ready nonetheless.

A referee stepped in. He'd gone to the trouble of putting on a white shirt and bow tie, too.

It was hot and sharp now. The evening was coming to its climax.

'I was shitting myself,' John would say later. He hardly showed it. He looked as mean and hard as any man there. The defences were up, and when they were, John was not a man to be taken lightly.

The buzz from the crowd grew louder. Many were commenting on the look of Billy. They hadn't heard of the Galway Bull, but they were just about to. The fight still felt a long way off if you were used to the preliminaries before a big scrap: the gowns, the parading of belts, the ring girls and the announcements. 'Let's Get Ready to Ruuuuuuuuumble,' as Mike Buffer will have it.

Instead, there was nothing, no prelude at all save for the icy, still, silent fractions of seconds before the bell rang, in which time everyone fell quiet. It was an unearthly hush, made almost tangible by the expectation behind it. Then the clanks of the bell sounded and there was a great whooshing, collective shout: 'YYEEEOOOAAARGGGGHHH.' John ducked out underneath the ropes and so did the second for Steve The Hammer.

The fighters quickly came together at the centre of the ring. Part of the reason why there were so many men here was this instantaneous high, a vicious, vicarious thrill of two men going at each other without ceremony. Billy and Steve spent precisely no time feeling each other out, testing each other's weight or finding each other's measure. This was a twelve-round, thirty-six-minute championship contest packed into four two-minute rounds. The spoiling and the showboating were for the pros, for the Vegas boys, for the Hameds and the Holyfields. They had both the time and the inclination, and Billy and Steve had neither.

They slammed together in a flurry of wild swings and fell against each other almost by default. Billy grabbed on to Steve and turned him around towards his own corner. It was an impressive show of his body strength, to take a fired-up, fifteen-stone man and realign him so quickly and easily. Steve was quickly back on to the balls of his feet, though, and the pair managed to shove themselves apart from each other. Then it happened. Billy took a step forward, threw out a lazy jab and left the whole left side of his head hanging up there like a bowling ball. Steve The Hammer swung a big haymaker of a right hand that landed flush on the jaw, bang on the button. It was a huge punch that travelled from way back behind his body and built up momentum all the way. Billy's thick neck barely moved back when the punch landed, its tightly wound muscles and sinews absorbing the shock. It was like hitting a tree trunk and expecting it to snap. Billy looked to have taken the punch, but further down his body the blow began to wreak havoc. His legs went, his knees nearly giving way underneath him. They buckled twice and each time he pushed himself back upwards again.

'I thought, "Fucking hell, he's going,"' said John Barnwell.

That would have been a new experience for Billy. He had never tasted the canvas before, and no one, Billy included, knew how his nerves and synapses would react. He could have fallen, or panicked, or blacked out altogether. Instead, he kept a grip on his senses.

Steve The Hammer followed through with a big left, looking to finish things right away, but somehow Billy ducked under it, a minor miracle of timing and balance under aching duress.

'I was so fucking proud of him at that moment,' John said. His gut instincts about Billy, that he was born to fight, like Duran and like Tyson, had been borne out. He had taken a massive shot, and he'd swallowed it like a champ. He was still in the fight.

Steve The Hammer, though, was encouraged too. His first big punch had landed, and although he might have expected it to take his man out, it had obviously done some damage, made some inroads.

Then Billy did what he always did. He moved forwards into the punches, facing the hard rain and taking shots on his arms and gloves. He used his weight to undermine The Hammer, to force him backwards through sweat and guts and will. He had little of the lateral movement that could have saved him some pain, but then he had strength and heart in abundance – and only eight minutes to make his mark.

The men around the ring wailed at him, urging him on.

They wanted a fight now, not a massacre. They had watched men crumble before Steve The Hammer and they were thrilled to be watching a fighter who hadn't.

The remaining one and a half minutes of the first were brutal. Once Billy had got close enough to overcome his lack of reach, he thrashed The Hammer in his ribs, the big roundhouse digs I'd seen from two feet away in the gym. He dug his toes into the floor as he threw them for extra purchase. The Hammer stayed upright, but his insides were being churned up as the punches drilled into him. They were landing everywhere in flurries as he covered up: on the biceps, the forearms, the elbows, the kidneys, the liver, some even further around the back.

Most unlicensed fights don't live up to the name. The lack of skill and heart will usually quickly lead to one man overpowering the other, finishing him quickly. But this one was different already. Steve The Hammer had done a bit, in the street and in the ring, and Billy lived to fight; he came alive when he was hitting and being hit, everyone could see that now.

Billy had rallied magnificently since his early setback. He kept up a high pace with his body shots, and Steve The Hammer was feeling his other-worldly power. Twice he managed to get into heavy clinches and limit Billy's effectiveness, and when the breaks were called by the referee, he moved back sharply and kept a distance between himself and his opponent by throwing out some thudding jabs. It was all at a cost, though. Billy's hours in the ring under John's supervision were paying big dividends for him. Steve was not used to fighting such a skilled boxer. He was unfamiliar with a man who could dictate the tactics of a fight to him. The scrap would now be conducted as much in the space between Steve The Hammer's ears as it would in the twelve square feet of the ring.

This was more than just a streetfight, and it would require more than just a streetfighter's mentality to survive and win it. The bell that sounded the end of the first two minutes was a relief to both men.

John jumped in to spray Billy with water and to get him to drink. He was shouting something into his ear but it was inaudible in the hubbub, even from ringside.

'I was just telling him to keep the fight in close,' he said later. 'To keep busting his body up and to stop him throwing long punches.'

The Hammer's corner was equally active. The Hammer shook his arms out and twisted from side to side to keep his body moving and stop it from stiffening. Both men were sweating and breathing hard.

They answered the rough bell for the second and went at each other again. It was withering. Billy was hellish to fight. He could swallow a shot and still pound away, and with his bulk and lack of height he was too low and too heavy to shove off easily. When The Hammer tied his arms up, as he did increasingly regularly, Billy shook his torso from side to side to free himself with the same motions that sharks use to twist meat from their catches. Again the round was being fought and won on the inside. Steve lacked the skills to keep Billy away from him, and he was suffering because of it. He was a good puncher and his height and length of limb gave him leverage, but he was used to fighting from a distance. Not many men had the strength or the determination to walk through his shots, but Billy always liked to take a punch in order to throw one.

His quiet words after sparring at the gym came back again: 'I love it . . .'

Billy fired a big, cuffing right hand over the top of Steve The

Hammer's guard, and it landed with a thud. It was followed by screams and exhortations from outside the ring.

'Fucking come on, Steve . . .'

'Get hold of it, Stevey boy . . .'

The crowd were being sucked further into the fight. John Barnwell was starting to go back on his prediction of trouble. The men here had seen fighters crack and were not lacking in appreciation for this one who hadn't. A few shouts for 'Paddy' were starting to sound out.

Billy was a crowd-pleaser. It was a visceral, thrilling fight, unlicensed or not. It wasn't dirty. There was no gouging or throwing, no kicks or wrestles or foul punches. The referee barely had to move in – not that he would have fancied getting between these two. There were true exchanges; both men were putting everything they had on the line. Here, the boundaries of sport were being crossed. The fighters were lacking nothing that the pros took with them to the ring. They were brave and strong and they were mentally hard. Either could have gone down under the pain and the pressure and the white heat of the expectation and the occasion, but instead they squared up and slugged it out. It was wonderful and full of dread, the 'terrible beauty' that Joyce Carrol Oates wrote of on seeing Mike Tyson early in his career.

There are times when you must question why you watch professional boxing, why it excites you when such devastating harm is at hand. It is a question even harder to answer with an unlicensed fight like this. The edge of illegality added to the fear and desperation, and yet . . . it was a thrilling fight, an awesome fight, filled with heart and human spirit. It was a sporting contest of the barest kind, but it was sport, with its techniques and constraints, and not a streetfight.

The two long, hard minutes of the second round drew to a close. Billy was clearly ahead. He stood in his corner, unmarked except for a reddening around his nose. His big chest heaved up and down, and he twisted his head around on his neck. John was rubbing him down, but he said little. Billy's fighting was eloquent enough. Here on this foreign field, he was winning the bout and the respect of the spectators. The positive energy was charging him up.

The third round was harrowing for Steve The Hammer, the hardest of his life. Billy doubled his effort. His trademark snorts were audible even above the general rumble, and his punches crashed home remorselessly. The dull thud of them sounded like a death knell. Steve was doing everything he could to keep Billy at bay, but he was sapped by the effort. His punches began to lose their weight and their purpose. Nothing could prepare a man for this sort of treatment in a fight. All that was left of Steve The Hammer was his pride – but that was considerable. He stood up and he took his beating. Twice he almost went down and twice the bulging ropes kept him on his feet. Billy, for his part, was finding it hard to finish the job. The adrenaline had taken its toll on his power, but still he battered away. When Steve was on the ropes, Billy would fire his sweet rights on to him, and each flurry provoked shouts and roars from the crowd, who were packing even more tightly around the ring.

After the two minutes were up, John Barnwell became concerned again about the crowd reaction. Steve The Hammer was hanging on by the merest of threads; only his heart was keeping him in it. He was a game boy, but Billy might win this inside the distance, and if he didn't he was well ahead anyway. 'I thought we would have to fight our way out of this one,' said John.

Although the crowd were screaming for a fight, howling for resolution and redemption of some sort, they were still behind The Hammer. But even the most one-eyed of the judges would have had to acknowledge that Billy was winning, and winning well. John was prepared to bundle Billy out of the ring and get him out of the doors and away as soon as the fight was done. He didn't care what way the matter was resolved – KO or by the opinion of the referee – just that he and Billy got out in one piece and a little richer.

The final two minutes began. Billy was hitting unanswered to the ribs and stomach, and all that was coming back the other way were some tired long shots. He slapped them aside. He was a relentless competitor and Steve The Hammer was a worthy recipient of his attentions. A contest of such rigour and angst was worth far more than the thousand pounds to the winner, or the cash that both would make from the tickets. They were no longer fighting for money, if they ever were. They were no longer streetfighters but boxers, licensed or not, and it was a contest full of courage and mutual respect.

For the final seconds, things got scrappy, then Billy ended with another strong assault. His punches powered home, short and sweet. The Hammer almost crumpled, but the last reserves in his sinews and nerve-ends kept him up. The bell rang out. It must have sounded like it came from another planet for Steve The Hammer. Those last two minutes had seemed deathless and inescapable, but escaped he had.

The ref stepped between the fighters and John Barnwell stuck his head through the ropes, expecting some sort of ugliness whichever way the result went. The ref pulled Billy and Steve to him, one on either side, and he gripped each of them firmly by the wrist. He hauled up Billy's arm – and also Steve's at the same time. A draw – the meanest, most one-sided draw ever fought out. Things stopped for a second. A draw? Then, to John Barnwell's disbelief and considerable relief, the front rows of the crowd were shouting up at the ring. They knew a winner when they saw one, and they were prepared to acknowledge Billy.

A chant began to rise from them, slowly at first, and then gaining momentum with each new voice.

'Paddy . . . Paddy!'

'PAD-DEE! PAD-DEE!'

'PAD-DEE! PAD-DEE!'

John reached Billy and pulled him out of the ring. The two fighters shot each other a look of acknowledgement, and then Billy was gone, away towards the back stairs.

* * *

Back in Billy's small changing-room, four or five men gathered around him. He looked drained, but also relieved. His face was as ruddy as it was after a day on the roads digging, and his body twice as weary, but he was barely marked. Even his nose had lost its redness. He had won the fight well, there was no doubt about that. The referee's opinion had become an irrelevance; Billy's legend had been made tonight, on the body of Steve The Hammer and in the minds of those who had seen him. Men had lost money in the nightclub, and there were stories that a couple had taken quite a hard fall on The Hammer, but somehow events had stretched beyond those considerations. They had seen something for their outlay; they had been rewarded by a contest of note, a fight that would be talked about for a long time to come. It would get bigger and bolder with each telling, too. That was part of the fun of this murky world. There were no video tape playbacks, no studio analysis, no newspaper reports. There was nothing left of the fight but memories, and they could become as selective as you liked. The fight had been an epic, and that's how it would be remembered.

Billy had quickly become the shy, self-effacing man of the gym again. He was drained of his aggression; it had been sated by his love of the fight. He had fought all kinds of men. He'd had to take baseball bats into rowdy pubs, he'd gone bare-knuckle for the gypsy championships and he'd survived brawls and jostles by the yard, but he somehow understood the boundaries of each. Billy was born to fight, and he had a natural instinct for what each fight required of him. He changed quickly.

John was still quietly amazed by how the evening had played out. He had certainly never seen a 'hometown' crowd react in the way it did. The referee had obviously thought he was doing the right thing by calling the match a draw. It would have been laughable to have given it to Steve, and, it seemed, dangerous to have given it to Billy. A draw seemed sensible, but now, John thought, Billy could count himself a little unlucky. Still, no one there could have doubted his dominance.

John's thoughts turned quickly to how he was going to get hold of the money. There had been a big turnout. Billy, he calculated, should receive at least a thousand pounds. He was still a little wary, especially about Trev's loose arrangement for its collection, but he had worked with him in the past and things had turned out okay. He decided quickly that he would go alone to collect the cash.

*   *   *

The van filled up again, slowly, as Billy and John's victorious crew left the nightclub. Now it was John rather than Billy who appeared preoccupied and tense. The money was on his mind. Billy had delivered his half of the bargain; now John, the trainer, cornerman, manager, matchmaker, must produce his. He and Billy spoke about the arrangements for the collection with the rest of the lads in the van. John wasn't really listening to anyone, though. He'd made his own plan. He would go to collect the money alone, with some back-up in the van. Billy immediately volunteered, but was quickly talked out of it. He was drained after the fight, even if the adrenaline that was still coursing through his veins wouldn't allow him to admit it. The last thing he needed was a potentially dodgy debt-collecting job. John advised him to wait in the van until the job was done.

'I wasn't fucking happy about it,' John admitted later. 'Going back to the gym, like. Trev's all right, though. I thought it would be okay, but I wasn't dead sure.'

The van ran smoothly over the late-night streets, only an occasional red light slowing its progress. Trev's gym was a couple of miles from the venue. It was a sweat and sawdust place, not unlike a fighter's gym, but instead of heavy bags and a battered ring it was loaded with large freeweights on bars, sloping benches and racks of steel that groaned under the poundages stored on them. Weight-belts hung off some of the racks. Instead of yellowing fight posters, the walls were lined with full-length mirrors. It was usually blindingly lit by strip lights, but at nights only a bulb at each end of the room remained on for security. The gym occupied a large single room above a shop that sold second-hand furniture. It could be entered two ways, one via a street door that sat in the recessed outer wall of the shop, and the other by external stairs at the rear of the shop.

John parked the van at the rear of the shop and took the back stairs. His large frame was silhouetted as he climbed. It was a melodramatic sight. He opened the door and walked through. He was in a dark passageway, but he walked along until he reached a rough wooden door. He pushed into the room and was surprised by the scene that met him.

He had gone into a small office area, which was brightly lit and choking with cigarette smoke. Trev was sitting in there, by a desk, and so were two or three other big men. They greeted John cordially, and at that moment, he said later, he knew that things would work out well. The men chatted for a while.

'Great fight, John, wasn't it?' Trev said.

John agreed.

'I've got to be honest, John, I thought Billy won it. It wasn't a fucking draw, that's for sure.'

John laughed. Trev had a pile of notes in a plastic bag on the desk in front of him, which he took out. He counted out the thousand again for John's benefit. While he counted he told John that they'd had to drag Steve from the ring. He was broken up inside.

John took the bag and shook hands with everyone again before he retreated back down the dark corridor.

'I stuck my head in there ready for whatever, but it didn't come to it, thank God,' he said later.

The night really couldn't have gone any better. The van filled back up with John, banknotes and laughter. It deposited its load at a pub and the relief was palpable. No one got too pissed. The night felt far too good for that. It didn't need any artificial enhancement for any of them. Billy was still quiet, but there was a calm about him, even though he must still have been racing inside. He went home and eventually slept. On Monday, Billy was back on the roads, digging out those yards.

* * *

Several weeks later, John went out to a club. Trev had put on another show and he'd asked John down. By chance, when John arrived, several of the men who'd been sitting with Trev in his office were on the door. They greeted him warmly. When he got inside, John heard someone call him over. It was Steve The Hammer.

'You've not got that Irish fucker with you, have you?' Steve grinned at John.

'Nah, you're all right,' John replied. 'Don't you fancy a rematch, then?'

'No chance,' Steve said. 'I was pissing blood for two weeks after that fight.'

Billy's name had been made by the encounter with Steve. The fight's epic nature, its fierce journey to the edges of organised brutality and the opportunity it had afforded both men to display spirit, courage and respect, both for themselves and for the fight game, had enhanced them both. Streetfighting had met boxing, and somehow boxing had won out – and so had Billy.

Billy had money. He had a nice place in London and a large holiday home, as well as the properties that he rented out, providing even more income. No one was going to back out on Billy for a week's rent. He really was like a mini Tyson. He hadn't needed to fight Steve, but he had wanted to. He didn't need to swallow that first big punch at the start of the fight and come back, but, again, he had. His opponent too had displayed a fighting heart as big as any. They might have been attracted by the cash, but when they were at the centre of that maelstrom it had counted for nothing. It was some fight. Steve The Hammer never entered a ring in anger again.

CHAPTER FIVE

LAS VEGAS

The Cat in the Hat must have been the skinniest man in Vegas. From the top of his skinny head, which was slotted into a flash fedora hat, to his long, skinny feet, which were encased in crocodile-skin loafers, he was as thin as a ghost.

He was playing dice on a craps table that was squeezed in a narrow gap of carpet between the slot machines and the Betty Boop bar in the MGM Grand Hotel, the world's largest casino. 'Oooooh . . .' he'd begin before every throw. 'Oooooh, lucky six . . . Ooooh baaaybeee, lucky siiiiiiiiixxx.'

As he reached the last long, sibilant 'sssiiiix', he'd hurl the two dice up the green velvet table and wait for them to bounce back from the far end. Every time they stilled, he'd let out a huge groan – 'Ooh . . .Ooh . . . OOOOOOOHHHHHH' – and then jump up, his slight body lifting a good three feet into the air and his bad teeth glinting gold under the low casino lights.

'Oh man, oh brother, these dice don't like me! These dice hate this brother! There ain't even no six on these dice!'

He'd got the small group around him excited, and in Vegas that's all it takes. Soon there were people jammed all around the Cat in the Hat as he dropped a few hundred dollars two hours before the richest fight of all time.

The Cat was hardly alone. The Betty Boop bar was buzzing at the arrival of a big-time American football player who had apparently been first or second pick in the annual college-players' draft. He was dressed in expensively casual silks and he was dripping in gold. Great chunks of it hung from around his neck and on his fingers. One ring was about the size of an end-zone and was covered in what looked like diamonds. He leaned across the circular bar with a fistful of dollars and ordered a bottle of Crystal champagne. It arrived in its pale bottle, with five glasses, at $200 a pop. It was the only drink going across the bar. On fight night, everyone in Vegas is rich, or at least making out that they are, or are just about to be. The barely dressed, beautiful girls were only at the tables where the Crystal was on tap.

The Betty Boop was the beating heart of the MGM. It was situated bang in the middle of the casino floor on a circular platform. You could reach it from whichever route you took into the casino: from the vast lobby with the huge green lion's head outside; from Studio Walk, with its designer boutiques and restaurants; from the elevators to the rooms, most of which had been 'comped out' as part of the opulent site deal struck by Don King when he brought the MGM's owner, Kirk Kerkorian, the single most lucrative property in world sport: 'Iron' Mike Tyson.

The Boop was a place to see and to be seen. I was only sitting in there because my friend Andy, who was in Vegas to write a travel piece for *The Guardian*, had been sitting at a table for a good part of the afternoon, waiting for the action to start. We should have known that all the luck in town had already headed out of the door and towards the distant canyons of Nevada. The Cat in the Hat had already found that out.

* * *

The sound filling the warm desert air seemed so out of place that I thought I was hearing things. After walking through the largest casino in the world, where the electronic pings and whirrs of the slot machines provided a ubiquitous backing track, the booming sounds of gospel music were a surprise.

Behind the MGM Grand Garden Arena, a 16,000-seat auditorium tacked on to the back of the largest lime-green building on earth, Don King, the street promoter supreme, the biggest hustler in a city that was full of them, had thrown up a giant white tent to act as a media centre for the third defining contest of his epic career. After The Rumble in the Jungle and The Thrilla in Manila came The Sound and the Fury: Tyson v. Holyfield II. Mike Tyson, the real one, not the white one back in south London, was in town to rebuild his legend by avenging his defeat at the fists of Evander Holyfield. And Holyfield was behind the MGM Grand, in a championship-sized ring inside Don King's carnival tent. The gospel music that was booming from a large ghetto-blaster was his, a heady mix of church singing and cheesy American rock that seemed to throw him into a semi-trance as he shadowboxed his way around the four corners.

Holyfield in Las Vegas appeared as dislocated as his music, a hard man of God in Sodom in the Sand, the 'Holy Warrior' that all of his merchandise – T-shirts, baseball hats, satin jackets, workout gear– proclaimed him to be.

Not since Muhammad Ali defeated George Foreman in Zaire had Don King sold a fight that so clearly delineated between good and evil. The righteous Holyfield, a truly God-fearing soul, had woven a hard spell over Tyson, the self-styled 'Baddest Man on the Planet', beating him badly when the pair had met in the same ring seven months before. By the eleventh round of the fight, the Baddest Man had looked like a chastened boy.

* * *

There was a fantastic line or two from the writer A.J. Liebling that kept flashing through my head every time I encountered Evander: 'When he walked to the ring, he was often smiling. He knew that when the heavyweight champion of the world defended his title it was a solemn moment, but he found it hard to forget how strong he was.'

Liebling had been writing about Rocky Marciano, but it could have been about the Holy Warrior. A smile played about his big, half-handsome, half-pug face every time he sat down to talk. His soft southern drawl added to his whacked-out, laid-back demeanour.

His routine was unalterable. He would arrive at the tent with his entourage after breakfast. They would make a circle, hold hands and then drop their heads and pray: Evander, his trainer Don Turner, a personal trainer, a masseuse, two bodyguards, even sometimes his lawyer, Jim Thomas. Someone would start up the ghetto-blaster and they would begin to stretch to the music. Holyfield always wore a white singlet and shorts and white boots. Only when you looked at his companions did you see the differences between mortals and gods. They jolted their bodies through the stretches; Holyfield's worked like a precision-engineered joint or piston. He swivelled at the waist and his shoulders spun while his legs remained still; he bent exactly in half and laid his hands flat on the floor; he reached up on tiptoe and twisted his head on his neck; and everything was balanced and proportioned, classically sculpted, fitted together in harmony by a benevolent maker. He didn't look like a heavyweight fighter. Heavyweights carried a bit of fat on the meat; they were muscley toughs like Tyson or gristly beanpoles like Akinwande. Their bodies were freakish, not perfect. They didn't have waspish waists and average-sized fists with long, slender fingers. But then everything about this man was different.

When the stretching was complete, Holyfield jumped up into the ring and lay down on his front while his masseuse dug her fingers into his back and down his arms. She rotated his wrists and pummelled his calves. The routine had grown as soothing as the massage itself; his mind was becoming as focused as his body.

Then came the hand bandages, which were cut to a perfect length and laid out on a table by the cornerman. They were fresh each time. Again the daily rhythms of their application marked the passing of time, the counting-down of the moments.

Then he would jump up and start to move to the music, circling the four corners and skipping from foot to foot as he did so. He'd begin to flick out punches and dodge imaginary returns, slipping his head from side to side, angling his body so that his heavy upper arms would absorb blows meant for his noble head. He would push out from one corner like this all the way across the ring, attacking smoothly before moving backwards just as silkily, firing on the retreat. He'd quickly begin to drip with sweat, like truly fit men do. And so his last few days before the fight went on, with this melding of body and mind orchestrated by his music.

When he had finished, Holyfield would wrap a new white towel around his shoulders, sit down on one of the benches erected to hold TV cameras for press conferences, and talk to whoever cared to come and sit beside him. That was when the Liebling line about Marciano started going through my head. Evander was always smiling. He was the most certain fighter, blessed with the steel of inner conviction. All boxers said they would win. They had to convince themselves more than anyone else. But Holyfield was certain of it, down in his core, even during the days when no one else gave him a prayer. 'I've already won,' he told me, his square jaw jutting upwards. 'I don't lose. I can't lose. The Lord never lets us down. We let ourselves down. I'm going to win. I wouldn't be here training if I wasn't going to win. Tyson is a tough fighter. I can't say he's the toughest fighter I've had, but he will definitely bring the best that you can handle.'

Holyfield seemed able to use his faith to toughen his body. He knew that he would be tested to the full by Tyson, that he would be hit and hurt as he had been during their first contest. But he never considered that he might yield. In the words of his favourite gospel song, he was a Mighty Man of God. The closer a fight came, the more intense he became in every aspect of his life. He made decisions. By his own count, he had proposed to three girlfriends as his big bouts grew closer. Before the first fight with Tyson, he had gone one step further and married a doctor, Janice Itson. Janice was now expecting his seventh child. Builders were completing work on his new home, the second-largest private residence in America.

As an amateur, Holyfield had been scared of being punched until he was knocked unconscious in a junior bout. After that, he was never afraid again. He developed a thing about bullies. Evander Holyfield never backed down again. He just smiled and kept on coming.

* * *

To the fight fraternity of insiders, outsiders, followers and fans in Las Vegas, Mike Tyson cast a shadow as deep as those thrown over the town by the mountains at sunset. Whether in person or as a rumour in the quietening late-night bars, he was ever-present. Tyson didn't like journalists; he didn't enjoy being questioned. That worked to his advantage in building his mystique. Since he had been released from jail, his image as the Baddest Man had grown in inverse proportion to the quality of his four opponents. His training camp was closed. After his defeat at the righteous fists of Evander Holyfield, he had cleared out some of his staff. Jay Bright, nominally his trainer, had been released. When Tyson fought Holyfield, Bright didn't even have an endswell in the corner for the bruises around Tyson's eyes.

'It was an easy decision. He was family,' explained Tyson darkly, 'and family is always first to go . . .' In his place was Richie Giachetti, a long-time associate of Don King who had a fat gut and a long knife scar across his cheek. Giachetti was a comedy Italian-American, gruff and surly. He claimed he was thrashing the lost skills back into Iron Mike.

No one believed him. Tyson trained himself. Older fighters tend to fall back on what they know, and Tyson was no exception. He would try to take Holyfield early, try to land those big bombs.

A month before the rematch with Holyfield was due to take place, Tyson pulled out with a cut eye sustained in sparring by a clash of heads. This sort of mishap seemed to follow Mike around. The postponing of bouts due to minor injuries like cut eyes and broken knuckles had been a feature of his career. They were inevitably accompanied by rumour and counter-rumour, and this one was no different. The truth was, no one knew. When Tyson was persuaded by Don King to go through an open workout for the benefit of the press in his white carnival tent, a kind of Iron Mike mania took hold.

His warm-up was perfunctory, and yet he looked quick and sharp. There was no sparring and no hitting back, just a session on the pads with Giachetti. Tyson fired out some combinations with a hard look of determination on his face. They fizzed into Giachetti's pads, forcing the fat Italian to hop smartly back-wards. Several of them drew applause. Tyson's black T-shirt quickly stained with sweat. Water poured freely from his hair-line down his face.

After the session, he travelled out past the Strip to Don King's large Vegas compound to take questions from the media. Tyson hated this, sitting in one of King's opulent living-rooms and being asked to bare his soul. He was barely audible sometimes, and he seemed aggrieved throughout most of the session. When someone asked him how he felt, he said, 'I've been taken advantage of all my life. I've been abused. I've been dehumanised. I've been humiliated. I've been betrayed.' His voice was little more than a sibilant whisper. 'I'm kind of bitter and angry at people about it. It keeps you sharp and witty to be revengeful, but it also keeps you broke. History proves that the only person in boxing who really struggles is the fighter.'

Tyson was more than aggrieved. He was forceful in his condemnations. His eyes hardened as he spoke. He was asked if he felt everyone was against him.

'Everyone is against us. We don't have nobody on our side. The courts are against us, the corporations are against us, the system is against us, the media is against us. We have nobody on our side and we're still fighting, we're still doing well.'

He continued, 'The fact is that you say we are monsters. You want the public to be afraid of us. They say we're not human. I think Don is a fool to have you over to his house to talk with you. You write these things and the people that know and love me read it and they feel awful.'

Tyson was both eloquent and convincing, and he managed to be those things and surly and threatening all at once.

'I'm a man,' he said. 'I'm not begging for people to love me. You don't know me. No one knows me. What has happened to me in my life makes me the person I am. I'm the only one that knows me.'

He spoke for a while about his children, and how he hoped

that the excitement of the streets with their collections of hustlers, chancers and charmers wouldn't hold the same appeal for them that it had for him. He said that they cried when they watched his defeat by Holyfield. He didn't seem like a bad man, or a bad father, but he didn't appear to have much peace in his life to fall back on, either.

* * *

His voice arrived before he did, and it was as recognisable a calling card as there was.

'Aha!' it went. 'Aha, my friends,' in the happiest, sunniest tones in the world. 'It's so good to be here. What's this?'

The voice fell silent in a way usually only employed in amateur dramatics productions. Then it started up again. 'Ahh, listen. Listen. It's the Sound. The Sound and the Fury.'

By now, the voice had emerged from the office and was in the main section of the big white press tent.

'I had the biggest fight of all time. I had two great champions, Mike Tyson and Evander Holyfield,' it continued. 'I had the MGM Grand Hotel, the best venue in the world. And I had no name for this Herculean contest! This meeting of pugilistic heroes! So I called up to heaven on my telephone. I spoke to my friend Billy Faulkner. I said, "Bill, I have the greatest fight of all time, and I have no name. Can you help?" And he gave me "The Sound". And I said thank you. Then the next night I called up to heaven on my telephone again. I spoke to my friend Ernie Hemingway. And I said, "Ernie, I've got the biggest fight of all time and I have no name. Bill Faulkner has given me 'The Sound'. Can you help?" And he gave me "The Fury". So there you have it. The Sound and the Fury. The name's by my friends Billy and Ernie, and I have the great honour and the great pleasure of bringing you the fight. Thank you all for coming.'

Don King grinned as he brought the curtain down on this ludicrous slice of hyperbole. It was a smile as wide as a hundred-dollar bill. His hair stuck straight upwards in its traditional style, only now it was more grey than black. He wore an expensively ugly short-sleeved safari shirt and shorts in matching crocodile green linen. On his wrist was a Rolex watch so studded with diamonds it was almost impossible to tell what the time was. On his feet were leather sandals. His toenails were huge and horny and no doubt expensively manicured. I looked at his long feet and thought about them kicking Sam Garrett to death in 1966. Sam Garrett's last words on this earth had been, 'I'll pay you the money, Don.'

King had been a streetfighter for all of his long and unlikely life. His history was as familiar to me as his face. Two men had died at his hands during his time as a small-time racketeer, the proprietor of a 'numbers' game, a kind of low-life lottery that he controlled in Cleveland. In 1954, he had shot Hillary Brown as Brown attempted to rob King's gambling club. It was ruled justifiable homicide. And on 20 April 1966, he quarrelled with Sam Garrett over a bet. The row moved from club to street, where King had stomped on Garrett until the police arrived and stopped him. Garrett died five days later, a horrible, lingering end. Amid allegations of corruption and a bought-off judge, charges against Donald 'The Kid' King were reduced from murder to manslaughter. He served three and a half years, and famously claimed many times that he used prison as his university. He devoured the literature that he has spouted back in his curious malapropisms ever since. Within five years of his release, and with no background in boxing, he had promoted The Rumble in the Jungle in Zaire.

That was the difference between King and the thousands of other hustlers. His extraordinary mind. He alone had the mental resources and personality to go from jail to convincing a tin-pot president, Joseph Mobutu, to provide $10 million to put on a boxing match. Thomas Puccio, a prominent attorney, had described King as 'by far the smartest man I have ever cross-examined'. Mike Katz of the *New York Daily News* once wrote, 'King is an evil genius. With his brain he could have done anything, even become president.'

His formidable skill as an orator was his other most reliable asset. With his innate cunning, King could blow linguistic smokescreens across seemingly clear-cut situations; he could bamboozle and cudgel and convince. He could deliver off-the-cuff speeches that went on for 45 minutes. He could calculate and assimilate the merits or disadvantages to him of any situation, and then find within his arsenal a response that would ensure that events swung his way. King liked to think of himself as a Machiavellian character; indeed, one of the nicknames he revelled in was 'Blackiavelli'.

But against that should be weighed two dead men and a long list of fighters who had endured indignity and hardship through their association with him. Twice he had stolen away Mike Tyson, the most valuable property in the sport. King thrived on chaos, and chaos was a fine and accurate description of the state Iron Mike usually found himself in. Firstly King had exploited the anguish and confusion Tyson felt over the death of his mentor Cus D'Amato to prise him away from Bill

Cayton. He gave Tyson a book, *Countering the Conspiracy to Destroy Black Boys*, of which he usually kept a dozen or more copies in his library, and shamelessly played the race card against men who had always treated Tyson well. When Tyson was released from prison, King had again ghosted past his adversaries to clarify Tyson's newly Muslim mind – with the aid of a cheque for $35 million. Tyson had been surrounded by Don King's influence ever since.

I found myself standing next to King, staring down at his feet and thinking about Sam Garrett. It seemed like it had happened a long time ago, in his first lifetime, before his existence took on the dimensions of a Homeric saga. Some successful people from dark backgrounds can cast them off. They have succeeded in spite of them. King, though, had succeeded because of his. Boxing *realpolitik*, with its ruthless backstabbings, its sudden and bewildering volte-faces, was a perfect arena for him to exploit both his brashness and his cunning.

A perfect example was Tyson's current trainer Ritchie Giachetti. Giachetti had been a small-time hood known to the FBI as 'Ritchie The Torch' because of his predilection for arson. He first met King in 1972, and he later began working as a trainer for Larry Holmes, then a King fighter. In 1982 he fell out with both King and Holmes and filed lawsuits against them. He had also offered to testify against King in an FBI investigation. King did not feel that Giachetti's threat was a light one and was rumoured to have taken out a contract on him with a known mobster called Frankie 'Flowers' D'Alfonso. Despite this, King had appointed Giachetti as trainer to Tyson twice: for his two scraps with Razor Ruddock, following the defeat by James Douglas and before his imprisonment for rape, and again for the return with Holyfield. That was heavyweight boxing. It never let a few lawsuits, a Federal investigation and a hitman stand in the way of business. Don King was once shot in the back himself. Metaphorical stabbings meant a little less to him after that.

The Don was on rambunctious form. He heard my accent and launched into his English shtick. 'A friend from England,' he began, his voice high with delight. 'How I love little England! Land of Bill Shakespeare and Frank Bruno . . . Brave men and true. God bless England.'

'Hello, Don.'

'Hello, my English friend.'

A huge beam. He began to answer some questions.

King's life and career seemed to be reaching a climax of sorts. He had spared nothing in his desire that 'The Sound and the Fury' should be the third great promotion of his career, the final part in a triumvirate begun by The Rumble in the Jungle and The Thrilla in Manila. The Sound and the Fury proffered a fight as intriguing as the previous two, and with an equal potential for greatness. It was also the first $200 million fight, a sum that not even King could have dreamed of when he raised $10 million for The Rumble back in 1974.

But there was more than just a defining heavyweight contest at hand for Blackiavelli. His empire was being assaulted from all sides. While Tyson had been champion, King had enjoyed control of the most charismatic fighter in the division and also its two premier titles, WBA and WBC. Now he had the fighter but not the belts, and if Tyson were to lose again King would be forced further from the centre of the sport. More seriously for his short-term future, King was facing a retrial on charges of insurance fraud, an indictment he had already survived once, when the jury acquitted him on a split decision. As a measure of his gratitude, King flew all twelve of them to Britain to see Oliver McCall fight Frank Bruno.

It was alleged that King falsified an insurance claim for $350,000 in lost training expenses to Lloyds of London following the cancellation of a fight between Julio Cesar Chavez and Harold Brazier in 1991. It was the FBI's case that King had never laid down the money in the first place, and had 'double-dipped'. It was a prosaic and casual crime, for what amounted to loose change for King. This was a man who has out-manoeuvred the FBI, giant corporations and entire Third World countries finding himself nailed for what amounted to little more than a speeding ticket.

At the original trial in 1996, King worked his bad magic on the stand. He gave the court his American Way speeches; he charmed them and made them laugh. 'Investigation is my middle name, baby,' he said when details of past inquiries were raised. Despite the years of painstaking investigation and hours of testimony, the Teflon Don had survived. Now he had been told to face it again.

I was in Vegas to write a story about Don King and his future. He was a little surprised when his 'English friend' piped up timidly about the Federal rap he faced, but the delay was only for a fraction of a second.

'I can't talk to you about that now, my English friend. You come and find me tomorrow . . .'

I was about to click off my tape machine when he erupted again.

'I perform better on a Federal indictment than other guys do when they're free,' he said suddenly and loudly. 'Think of what I could do if I had liberty and justice for all. I'm indicted and

I've held 47 championship fights. It's kill the nigger, dig him up and kill the nigger again! They indicted me when I was the one who got shot in the ass! They want to get rid of me cos they can't beat me. They can't stand a nigger doing well. I'm a nigger with a stacked deck. They got me with a cold deck.' He looked serious for a minute, and then he beamed again.

'Come and find me tomorrow, my English friend. I'm sure I'd get better justice in your country . . .'

* * *

It was a Friday, the last before the fight. Bally's and the MGM ran a monorail in a rare spirit of casino co-operation. It saved you walking up the strip and dropping into anyone else's gaming hall or designer franchise or steak joint. In the big white tent, Don King was mobbed by TV crews and reporters. He showed no signs of recognising his new English friend.

The weigh-in for Tyson and Holyfield was scheduled for 4 p.m. in the MGM ballroom. King had learned his lesson from the weigh-in of the first fight, which was held in the Grand Garden Arena itself, on a temporary stage in front of the ring apron. It had been ugly. Tyson's menace and bad vibes spilled over into the crowd. There were two fights, one involving Tyson's former trainer Teddy Atlas.

I got to the ballroom early, not too hopeful of finding Don King in a position to tell me any more about his retrial, or about anything else. The ballroom was large and high-ceilinged, and a low dais had been put up at the far end. In the middle of it stood the big iron scales for the weigh-in. Down the left-hand edge of the room ran a crush barrier behind which a few fight fans would be allowed to stand and watch.

An hour or so passed. The room filled. I sat by Budd Schulberg, who wrote the movie *On the Waterfront*. He was a wise old head, and his money was with the champ. King flitted back and forth across the stage, which was separated from the main floor by more barriers. Then Holyfield's team arrived, surrounding their man. Evander was cheered all the way in.

'Who's the Man? Who's the Man?'

'Evander! Evander's the Man!'

Then it was Team Tyson's turn. First came Steve Fitch, better known as Crocodile. Crocodile was the biggest mouth in Vegas, and that was saying something. He had no job other than to walk around the hotel shouting things like, 'Guerrilla warfare . . . It's Wake-Up Time! It's Tyson Time!' He always wore shades, a bandanna, combat fatigues and a black jacket that had 'Hated by Most. Liked by Few. Feared by All.' written across the back. He seemed to have spawned a couple of little crocodiles, who followed him around, shouting his slogans. Then came the rest of Team Tyson: Richie Giachetti, John Horne and Rory Holloway. Horne and Holloway were a pair of King henchmen who were employed as Iron Mike's co-managers. Holloway had been Tyson's friend since the Catskill days and was a chubby, nondescript character. Horne was a more standard chancer, a stand-up comedian who had introduced Tyson to Robyn Givens. Horne had a high-pitched voice and a volatile temper.

Then Tyson himself, shaven-headed and squat and loaded with menace. His presence never failed to galvanise any room he entered. He was darkly charismatic, a mass of contradictions, a hugely complicated man who had led an unimaginable life. Sometimes he would do nothing to disguise his boredom and disdain for people. He would put his head in his arms and sleep while writers asked him questions. Other times he would talk with a moving eloquence about himself. He was America's bogeyman, The Baddest Man on the Planet, and yet he was strangely, ridiculously, vulnerable.

After he had been beaten by Holyfield in their first fight, he attended the press conference in Don King's big white tent and made a speech in which he acknowledged Evander as the better man and apologised to him for some of the pre-fight remarks he had made about him. Then he said, 'It's not how you lose, it's how you come back.' When he sat down again, the tent full of hard-bitten journalists stood up and applauded. When people began to leave the tent, he remained sitting at the dais for a long time. I finished making my notes and left by the side exit. Iron Mike got up at the same time and left by the same exit. We were walking along together, side by side, twenty yards from anyone else. It seemed strange that, after a fight of such significance, watched by half the world, he should be alone and walking along, looking for his ride home.

'Bad luck, Mike . . .'

He looked up and half smiled.

'Thanks,' he mouthed, the word barely solid enough in the air to be audible.

He had long grooves in his forehead where he and Holyfield had clashed heads for eleven fierce rounds, and he was holding a white towel that he had been pressing to his bruises. He had shaved after the fight, and put on a collar and tie. He seemed just like a little boy. Then his wife Monica got out of a green Land-Rover and walked up to him. He wrapped his arms right around her, and she whispered softly in his ear. Then he got into the Land-Rover and she drove him home, steering the car towards the dark desert.

That was part of Tyson's intrigue. He was so many different men. He had trained hard for the rematch. When he stripped off to be weighed in, his chest was smooth and flat, like marble. He was ripped, far more muscular than usual, and a little lighter. Holyfield too was magnificently conditioned. They were equal in size at 218 lbs. Don King grabbed both men by the wrists and lifted their arms skywards. Tyson wrenched his arm away angrily.

The rest of the weigh-in went off without incident. I found Don King down by one side of the dais, where he was being presented with a painting of himself. It was a montage, with a central portrait surrounded by cameos of King with his great fighters, a style popular with boxing artists everywhere. The artist was a young man and the presentation was being co-ordinated by a fey old white guy who looked like a butch Quentin Crisp.

Don King was apparently delighted with his gift.

'Ladies and gentlemen,' he yelled. 'We have had Michelangelo. We have had Rembrandt, and we have had Picasso. Now we have this young man. Just look at this work of art. It could hang in the Sistine Chapel.'

The people gathered around laughed at King's brio. His use of the language was the stuff of legend. The malapropisms flowed – his best during the fight build-up was 'In the land of the Cyclops, the one-eyed man is king' – as did his capacity to invent words. His newest, directed, of course, towards the FBI, was 'insinuendo', at once nonsensical and hugely appropriate.

When he had received his painting, he stepped over towards me.

'Don, what about the Chavez trial?' He was instantly attentive, replying without even blinking.

'My government wants to put me in jail. They're going to say I stole $200,000 from a victim who doesn't exist! They put me up in front of a jury of eleven white folks and one black last year and the white folks said, "He didn't do it!" But then it's, "Let's dig the nigger up and kill him again."'

His hair stood up straight, electrified by the sheer charge coming from the motion of his mouth. He cranked the voltage up another notch and his voice got high and shouty. He leaned in closer.

'I'm calling on everyone who's fair-minded. I paid thirty million in taxes last year. They want me for two hundred thousand! Black kids want to see a hero. I'm a voice in the wilderness. The betterment of this great country, America, the greatest nation on earth, is my goal. Life, liberty and the pursuit of happiness.'

As he finished this mighty mix of invective and hokum, he rocked back in his crocodile-skin sandals.

'Tell it like it is, Don,' a man yelled admiringly. 'Yes sir! Tell it like it is . . .'

'This is not a criminal offence, man. Lloyds of London get on to me, or I get on to them and go, "Let's negotiate." They take back a hundred grand or two hundred grand. It ain't nothing. I'm back on trial because they couldn't get me on anything else. They're gonna make sure they get my black ass, but I'm a Yankee Doodle Dandy, a proud boy, born on the fourth of July. If they put me in jail, I'm gonna walk round the yard in a circle waving the flag.'

This was a typical King smokescreen. He was, of course, fully aware that fraud *is* a criminal offence in America. Then he played one of his regular aces.

'They want me because they can't stand a nigger doing well,' he hollered. 'Larry Holmes said he got more money with me stealing from him than he did getting a hundred per cent from anybody else. I'm just a guy on the street. All these great white folks, they've been to Harvard and Yale, Oxford and Cambridge, and they can't make what I make. I ain't got no machine gun! I ain't making no one work with me.'

By now, we were surrounded by journalists, and there were plenty of admirers urging him on. 'We got a Frankenstein in this nation. It's called racism. We can't allow our children to feed this Frankenstein. They are our future. You got Bill Cosby. His son Ennis shot in cold blood. Then you got a grandson burns up Betty Shabazz.' Betty Shabazz, the widow of Malcolm X, had just been murdered in an arson attack.

'What that tells us,' King lectured, 'is that it don't matter if you're black or white, rich or poor, your life is worthless. We gotta have Christian values. We gotta change people's opinions. Instead, they're trying to put me in jail for $200,000 when I could give you $200 million. What are they doing? Give me community service! Make me pay some huge sum to charity. But no, every black hero, they gotta assassinate.

'I'm from the 'hood. I know what's going on. It ain't about doing wrong, it's about doing right. I said, I'm gonna play the game like the white folk. I got a motherfucking PhD in that game and now they want to put me in jail. I'm willing to die for America. I've got to stand up for it. I ain't gonna let them scare me about going to jail. I've been there. I don't give up because they lock the door. I'm the King of the Dark. I ain't got no axe to grind. I'm a nigger. If I'm successful, deal with me. If I'm unsuccessful, kick me, but don't try and get me outta the way with this shit. It's a victimless crime.'

He stopped yelling. Several people applauded. Good luck to the FBI. They had their work cut out.

After the weigh-in there was a hastily convened meeting of the Nevada State Athletic Committee, the men who controlled boxing in Las Vegas. There was a long-standing suspicion, which was not without evidence, that they were an organisation in Don King's pocket. Team Tyson had made a late complaint about the choice of referee for the fight. They had threatened to pull out unless Mitch Halpern was removed and another official put in his place. It was a dramatic sign that Tyson was weak mentally. He didn't need to be fussing about the referee with a day to go. Across the Sportsbooks in the casinos, his odds immediately lengthened, although he remained favourite against all of the evidence – except the flawed myth of his invincibility as The Baddest Man.

The appeal was farcical. Don King was anxious to keep favour with his erratic meal ticket and so he spoke in favour of the withdrawal of Halpern. John Horne screamed at the commission in a high-pitched voice.

'You are disrespecting Mike TYSON!'

The Team Tyson case was that Halpern had done nothing to stop Holyfield's roughhouse tactics in their first fight. Tyson felt that he had been unfairly treated and he had said so afterwards. Now he was concerned that Mitch Halpern might not be totally impartial. The commission quickly rejected the appeal.

Don King's mood was blackened by the hearing. The King of the Dark stalked away. The fey old man with the painter friend asked him to stop for a photograph with the artist and his picture. 'Not now,' he hissed, and was gone.

By the next morning, Mitch Halpern had decided that he

didn't want to referee the fight, and he was replaced by the veteran Mills Lane. It was not difficult to imagine that the King of the Dark had been busy once again under the cover of the cool desert night.

*   *   *

By the late Saturday afternoon, every gangsta from Los Angeles seemed to be in the MGM lobby. Rumour and counter-rumour circulated about who was in the casino and who wasn't: this ball-player, that rapper. We sat in the Betty Boop bar watching the Cat in the Hat wave goodbye to his cash. The Boop was the place to be seen for Tyson's crew, and the nature of Iron Mike's appeal in America was obvious. Just as he had been ostracised by the mainstream public, so he had been embraced by the street class, the underclass and the dislocated. He was one of theirs, and they loved and revered him. He was the Baddest Man, a man who had done hard time on the strength of a dubious conviction, when a prominent white man, William Kennedy, had faced similar charges and been acquitted just weeks before him. Tyson was what America had made him, the flip side of the American Dream, distrusted and disenfranchised, feared and loathed and badly misunderstood. He was the human equivalent of gangsta rap: aggressive and impenetrable to the outsider, eloquently understandable to his audience. The men and women who followed Tyson had lived his life too. He represented the divisions by race and wealth in America; he was the ghost from the ghetto. He was ostentatiously rich; he bought mansions and motors, jewellery, gold

115

teeth, designer clothes. He wore his money as the badge of his achievement, just as his followers did. He refused to care what other men thought of his lifestyle. Like his personal hero, Sonny Liston, he had an air of premature doom about him. He had often said he couldn't imagine himself growing old. He was from a world where early death was normal and acceptable, where life was hard and violent and short. He faced his end with acceptance, just as many of his fans did. They were alive now, though, and so was the Betty Boop.

The King of the Dark's undercard for the fight was uninspiring. Julio Cesar Chavez limped to his one hundredth win, a slow points victory over Larry LaCoursiere. Christy Martin, 'The Coalminer's Daughter' and King's current fancy as a carnival attraction, won an untesting bout against Andrea De Shong by stoppage. There was no atmosphere until nine o'clock drew near. Then, suddenly, from the far right-hand corner of the Grand Garden Arena came a long 'HISSSSSSSSSS' from the crowd and the clanking of feet on metal steps. They were standing because he was here at last, the Baddest Man, the Bogeyman: Iron Mike.

The Crocodile led him in. A small army of people bounced up and down around him to blaring rap music, Public Enemy's 'Welcome to the Terrordome'. Tyson had a white towel over his sloping shoulders, his head poking out of a freshly cut hole. Black shorts, black boots, no socks. He rolled his head around on his neck to release the tension, just as he had done every time he had ever made this walk. He placed his arms on the shoulders of the man in front and bounced up and down, from foot to foot. He climbed the steps to the ring. Above him, the spotlights flashed on and off. He ducked through the ropes and sidestepped his way across the ring, pleased to finally be there.

The Public Enemy tune stopped, and a huge, throaty roar echoed around. It was hard to tell if it was for or against Tyson.

The monitors at ringside and the big screens above the ring showed Holyfield leaving his dressing-room. He too was constantly rotating his head on his neck, and he had tears streaming down his cheeks. Along with his proposals of marriage, this was another staple of Evander's big fights. The tears were a sign of the intensity of his emotions, of his desire to win. He came to the ring to the sound of his favourite gospel rock song, 'Mighty Man of God'. He was in purple and white, and he had his reference to Philippians 4:13 on his shorts ('I can do all things through Him, which strengthens me'). Don King joined everyone in the ring. The fighters tried to keep moving while the introductions were made and the national anthem was sung by a young woman. Don King, the Yankee Doodle Dandy born on the fourth of July, joined in.

The ring cleared and the fighters moved forwards to hear instructions from Mills Lane. His instructions were the best of all the referees because he closed them with his trademark line, which he shouted rather than spoke: 'LET'S GET IT ON . . .'

The bell rang and the fight began. I watched Tyson closely for any sign that he still had Holyfield's dominance boring into his mind. He didn't show any fear, but he got thrown out of the first clinch and took a couple of good, rough shots. He was wary of Holyfield's head, and Holyfield kept it down low, drilling in, determined to impose himself physically again. Tyson was way below his best. In fact, his best was ten years gone. The lateral movement that had made him so hard to hit and stop had been lost. He was well conditioned but badly trained. He seemed to have no gameplan beyond getting lucky with a big shot. He had been a relentlessly bleak fighter, swarming over his opponents, cutting up from underneath them with his low centre of gravity, breaking their bodies and their minds, their spirits and their hearts. His first trainer under Cus D'Amato, Teddy Atlas, thought that Tyson's style would not enable him to last into his thirties as a fighter. It was a young man's style. Atlas called Tyson 'a comet, not a star'.

Atlas had been asked how he thought Tyson would do against Holyfield this time. He had replied, 'Holyfield, by disqualification.'

The first was all rough stuff, and Tyson seemed to be holding his own. Holyfield appeared intent on using his head to hurt Tyson. The bell rang and both fighters stalked back to their corners. Giachetti was screaming at Tyson to watch his head when Holyfield came out of the clinches, and it proved to be prophetic advice. In the second, they went into a close exchange and Holyfield lifted his head sharply on the break. It cracked into Tyson's brow with an audible THUNK. Tyson reeled back, shocked. A large cut had opened above his eye. Blood immediately began to run down one side of his face in three thin streams. It looked black against his dark skin. He turned to Mills Lane and complained bitterly but the crowd roared at him to shut up and fight. At the bell Tyson hunched in his corner, his mind breaking, blood already on him, his worst fears in attendance after six quick minutes. He squealed out in pain when his cuts man shoved an adrenaline bud into the gash under his low brow. Giachetti got right in Tyson's face, shouting. His gut brushed against Iron Mike's knees. Lane came over and told Tyson that the butt had been accidental.

When he came out for the third, Tyson had no gumshield in. Holyfield himself pointed it out to Mills Lane, and Giachetti rinsed one down and put it in Iron Mike's mouth. Tyson began the round well. His combinations were beginning to take effect. Holyfield could only counter by hitting Tyson's arms and holding. Then Tyson caught Holyfield with a big right, the best shot he'd managed in two fights and fourteen rounds against him. Holyfield rocked back on his heels and then clinched. Tyson rested his head on Holyfield's shoulder. I looked at Holyfield and saw that he was hurt but all right. He was taking a breather. Then he leapt up in the air as Mills Lane called the break and everyone around me jumped up too. Holyfield had turned his back on Tyson, and Tyson tried to wave him in. Then he shoved Holyfield into the ropes. The hack next to me was screaming at the top of his voice. The words seemed to come out in slow motion.

'Jesus fucking Christ, he BIT HIM! Did you see that? He fucking BIT HIM!'

Holyfield was pawing the side of his head with his glove. Blood was running down from his ear. The top part of it was missing. Mills Lane walked to the judges and deducted two points from Tyson's score, one for the bite and one for the push. Holyfield spoke to Tyson: 'C'mon, man, you've gotta chance here,' in reference to the punch that had shaken him.

The Sound and the Fury had become a savage mess. Both men had slipped away from the rules of the contest and also from the spirit of it, Holyfield with his use of the head and Tyson with his mouth.

The crowd were watching the replays of the bite on the big screens suspended above the ring. Roars of shock were rippling down the stands. Down in the corner where the boxers had come into the arena, a fight broke out between two sections of fans. The police restored order with riot sticks. It was becoming a wild and ugly night at the MGM Grand Garden. Licensed or not, The Sound and the Fury was a streetfight, give or take $200 million.

Everybody was standing, screaming, yelling, hooting, losing it. It had become inconceivable that the fight would continue for much longer. It would soon reach its awful conclusion. Tyson spat out his gumshield and bit Holyfield's other ear. Mills Lane threw him out. Immediately, the ring was full of people: fighters, trainers, cornermen, officials, policemen. Everyone pushed and shoved forwards. Tyson was in one corner with his bad eye almost shut. He was trying to punch out two Las Vegas cops. On his face was a look that combined violent intent with confusion and a touch of temporary madness. John Horne was screaming at anyone who would listen. Rory Holloway looked podgy and unsure, a man drowning.

Evander Holyfield ducked out of the opposite corner and was escorted away. Nobody announced to the crowd what had happened. The fight was over, but no one had told them why. Don King stood in the ring, his big face as grey as his hair. His dreams for another fight to match The Rumble in the Jungle or The Thrilla in Manila had turned to blood and dust. This fight would make a legend of another kind. Tyson was somehow manhandled out of the ring and back to the dressing-rooms.

* * *

I ran all the way back to Don King's white carnival tent for the post-fight press conference. Even men who had been covering the fight game for many years were in shock. Their laughter was a little too forced, their *bonhomie* misplaced. Holyfield had been taken to hospital to have the top of his ear re-attached. Tyson was pulled from his dressing-room by a TV reporter. People surrounded him. He wore a woven shirt in tribal colours which was unbuttoned to the middle of his chest. He had put on a chunky necklace, and a strip of instant stitches had been stuck above his eye. Unused energy burned from him, and sweat gathered at his hairline. His eyes were screwed up with emotion. He was utterly menacing, a force cut loose. His voice was at the top of its range, his little-boy lisp more pronounced. His head rolled from side to side as he talked.

'He butted me in the first round and in the second round again,' Tyson said. 'He kept going down and coming up on me. This is my career. I have children to raise. I have to retaliate. He butted me. I complained in the first round and nothing was done. He's not tough. Look at me. I have one eye. I'm ready to fight him now. He didn't want to fight. Regardless of what he did, I did address it. Look at me. My kids will be scared of me.'

His voice was almost pleading as he said the part about his kids. People just laughed and scoffed. I thought that the stuff about the butts was true enough.

Mills Lane came into the tent and sat down to take questions. He was a small, square man who worked as a circuit judge. He had been a Marine in his day. He said that he gave Tyson the benefit of the doubt after the first bite but had to throw him out after the second. Everyone cheered him for his guts.

An hour or so passed. King's people produced photostats of some comments Holyfield made on his way to the hospital. I spoke to Budd Schulberg, who shook his head sadly and said that he never thought he'd see the day. He looked genuinely hurt.

Don King was so quiet it was almost impossible to tell that he was there. He spoke at half the speed that he usually did. His voice was slow, like it was being played back on a tape recorder with low batteries. Suddenly he looked every one of his sixty-seven years. His jowls sagged and his hair refused to assume its usual cockscomb. He was like a man whose jail sentence had already begun. Even the King of the Dark had had his dreams shattered. He was almost lost for words, but even now he retained enough awareness of his position to hedge his bets.

'The head butters were there. Prior to that, they took a point away. They told them to watch the head butts before the fight started. I have to see the replays before I can comment further.'

'Don,' someone asked, 'should Tyson be paid?'

'Yes, they should be paid,' he replied. 'They came and fought.'

* * *

Andy and I walked together back into the MGM. We were trying to rationalise what had happened, but it defied rationalisation. Events had got way out of control. None of the unlicensed bouts I had seen had crossed the line in the way that this fight had. The air in the MGM still reeked of violence, of business not yet concluded.

We cut down Studio Walk, past the designer boutiques and the restaurants. A wave of people came running around the corner towards us. One woman was screaming as loudly as she could. She slipped on the floor and almost got trampled by some of the others coming along behind her.

'They're shooting, man, they're shooting!'

Glass began to smash against the floor in the restaurant. The diners were turning their tables over and crouching behind them. Andy and I jumped over a knee-high brick wall and dived into the restaurant. We ducked down behind a couple of upturned tables. Screams rang out from the people scattering to avoid the gunshots. Visions of the Mike Tyson–Buster Mathis fight ran through my head. The rap singer Tupac Shakur had been assassinated in a car on Las Vegas Boulevard a few hundred yards from the MGM Grand.

I stayed crouched down behind the table for two or three minutes. I was expecting someone to come around the corner firing, but there was no one, and there were no gunshots to be heard. I got up. The restaurant was wrecked.

In the casino, gaming tables had been overturned. There were stacks of thousand-dollar gambling chips lying on the floor. Some people were picking them up and shoving them in their pockets.

The Las Vegas police took control of the lobby and the casino entrance. I walked out of the main entrance and found a spokesman for the Vegas cops. He said that someone had popped a champagne cork and that a couple of crush barriers had turned over. People had mistaken that for gunshots and panicked. But the crowds leaving the MGM were not the kind of people who would mistake a popping champagne cork for a gunshot. I wouldn't mistake a popping champagne cork for a gunshot, and I was new in town. But gunshots at a $200 million fight were bad news for Las Vegas, the family holiday centre.

* * *

The riot in the MGM was over. The casino floor was closed by the police, with catastrophic consequences for the finances of the hotel. Across Las Vegas Boulevard, the gaming tables and the slots in the New York New York had suffered a similar fate. Andy and I walked back through to the deserted Grand Garden Arena. We stopped for a moment on the upper balcony, looking down on the ring. There was no one anywhere among the rows of seats save for a couple of journalists still at the ringside benches. One was Mike Katz, of the *New York Daily News*. A cleaner was slowly putting discarded cups and wrappers into a sack that was held open on a trolley.

I went down the steel stairs of the stands and across the floor. My footsteps rang out. It was quiet and still, ghostly.

Mike Katz smiled mournfully as we went past.

'Whadda guy, eh?' He shook his head – with difficulty, as his neck was in a brace.

We approached the ring. I stood on the three steep iron steps by the ringpost for a while, and then ducked between the ropes and got inside the squared circle, alone but surrounded by cataclysmic history. The ring bounced under my feet. There was a surprising amount of give in the boards, lots of sponge in the mat around the huge 'Budweiser: King of Beers' logo across the middle of the ring. I stood in Tyson's corner. There was a lot of blood on the floor, which was now almost black against the bright blue canvas. Then I stood in Holyfield's corner: less blood, the same colour. We left. Outside, the lights of the city burned, and beyond them the mountains stood like shadows on a soft horizon. I looked out at them and wondered where Mike Tyson was now, and what havoc he might be wreaking.

*   *   *

Two days later, the former Baddest Man on the Planet read a prepared statement to the Nevada State Athletic Commission in the ballroom next to the arena where the weigh-in had taken place. He wore a white suit and had a large strip of tape on the cut above his eye. He lisped his way through it like a little boy. They took away his boxing licence indefinitely, with leave to appeal after one year. When he walked out of the ballroom, still surrounded by his team, Mike Tyson was the most famous unlicensed fighter in the world.

CHAPTER SIX

MISMATCH

Nibbs had been a pro, he said. His name was Jimmy Ryan, but everyone called him Nibbs. When he fought, he had billed himself as Jimmy 'His Nibbs' Ryan. He took three fights, 'and I didn't come second,' he said with a smile. But the pro game was hard going for Nibbs and for lots of other fighters like him. Small-hall boxing was dying in England; it was out on its feet. The journeyman professional couldn't get the fights. Nibbs wasn't a knockover, so some of the matchmakers weren't keen on putting him up for one of their prospects. But he had no big promoter queuing for his services either. He didn't have much in the way of star quality, but he was a rough, tough, hard man, an awkward customer. He just couldn't get the work. His last fight had been as a late replacement at the York Hall in Bethnal Green. The phone rang at four thirty and he was in the ring by eight o'clock, outpointing a ponderous middleweight over six rounds. He netted £250. In eleven months as a professional boxer he earned £950. 'His Nibbs' retired because, he said, he couldn't afford the brain scan he needed to renew his licence, even by dipping into the dole money and housing benefit he was claiming.

Nibbs lived in White City, in a place he called the Basin. The Basin was on one of the tired overspill estates in the holes between the city and the suburbs that had been hauled up in optimism and then drowned in helplessness and dread. Nibbs's flat, which huddled up next to endless serried lines of identical others, had two living rooms, a sliver of kitchen and a bathroom. The only natural light battled its way gamely through a yellow plastic temporary window. A mate had been due round for the last two weeks to put in a new piece of glass, but he'd been inexplicably detained elsewhere, Nibbs explained.

'I dunno what's happened to 'im,' Nibbs said. 'Good as gold, he is usually.' He had an air of hurt bafflement about him that had accompanied the small defeats in his life. Whenever he had been let down, when fights hadn't materialised or a sparring partner hadn't shown or a 'bit of business' had failed to come his way, Nibbs would look sadly at you and say, 'I can't understand it,' and he really couldn't.

He wasn't particularly worried about the plastic window. He didn't have much worth nicking and, anyway, someone would be round to tell him in which pub he could buy it back on the cheap. Not too many people messed with Nibbs. He was a part of the furniture in the Basin.

I drove there to meet him and I stopped to ask directions at the mouth of the estate. There were a few kids standing around, looking up at the stone pillars of the flyover. The biggest looked about eight or nine years old. I wound the car window down. He didn't answer my question at first, and when I asked him again he stared for a while and then said, 'I've got a knife.'

When I told Nibbs, he just laughed.

Nibbs was born near to the Basin on the same estate, and he figured on boxing being his only chance of a ticket out. The end of his professional career had left him bitter at the management of a sport in decline.

'I can't understand it,' he said as he wedged himself into his little strip of kitchen and wrung the last dregs from a teabag by grinding it against the side of the mug with a spoon. 'I mean, if I'm rubbish, I can get a fight, right? As many as I want, right, if I'll just fall over. But I won't. I ain't going to lie down, but I ain't going to rip up any trees either if I can't get the fights. Frank Warren seen me one night and he don't fancy me. I got told if I won I'd be up for a fight with one of his boys. But he's seen me knock this kid down and he don't fancy me doing it to one of his.'

Frank Warren had become the bane of Nibbs's life. The perceived slight at the fight had been fed on so much angst, it had taken on the dimensions of paranoia. There would be no upward sweep in Nibbs's life, no way out of the Basin. Someone who trained with him had told me that Frank Warren hadn't even been in his seat while Nibbs was fighting.

Nibbs had been at the gym one night when one of the trainers he knew well enough to say hello to had offered him £400 to come and have a scrap with a man he'd never heard of, at an unlicensed show in Peckham. Nibbs was sure he knew of every half-decent fighter in London, so he'd edged the price up to £450 and taken it on. He knocked the man out with his first punch. It was easy money for Nibbs, easier than any he'd earned as a pro.

Now Nibbs had a new career, and, as he told me, 'There ain't going to be no promoters or no one else blocking me.'

Nibbs had three more fights within two months. He'd started going down to Maidstone, where there was a warehouse that was used for unlicensed boxing every Saturday night. He was in the game.

* * *

The phone went late one night and it was Nibbs. 'There's a big show on up in Shepherd's Bush on Friday,' he said. He sounded excited. 'Bloke called me up today. Wants me as a reserve for one of the fights. I get £20 for going down and I get £400 if one of 'em doesn't show up and I get the fight.'

Nibbs told me that I could come along with him if I wanted to, as long as I was at his place by six o'clock.

The show was in the back room of a huge Victorian pub. The manager had drawn some big double doors across to keep the back room shut away, and there were two big men on the door. They both knew Nibbs.

'You on tonight then, Nibbsy?'

'Reserve, mate,' smiled Nibbs. 'So I hope one of the fuckers don't show.'

It was packed inside. The ring had been put up towards the back of the room, so that people could only stand around three sides of it.

'Looks a bit of a fucking small ring, that,' thought Nibbs. 'Ain't gonna be anyone running away tonight. No Gees, I don't reckon.'

'Gees' were Gee-ups. They came along every once in a while in unlicensed fighting. The fights looked real to any 'mug punters', but the fighters were carrying each other.

Nibbs looked around for Jimmy, another Jimmy, who was the promoter. He found him in the pub kitchen, where he'd set up shop. People were flying in and out.

'They've both shown up, Nibbs,' said Jimmy straightaway. He handed Nibbs a couple of tenners and ignored his disappointed look.

Nibbs decided to hang around and watch the two lads who'd deprived him of a fight. They were third on. The first two fights were scrappy, and they both went the distance of four two-minute rounds. The crowd grew a little restless.

'See these blokes here,' said Nibbs, looking around him, 'these blokes would have used to have gone to the small-hall shows. But they're finished. Big promoters and that lot ain't interested, and the local man, the small promoter, he can't make the cash. That's why unlicensed has got so big.'

The fight started. The men looked to be about Nibbs's size. They flew at each other from the bell, neither giving an inch. They were too close together to gain any leverage with their punches. Nibbs looked disgusted even before one of them hit the deck after walking on to a simple left cross. He could probably have beaten both of them at the same time.

Jimmy the promoter was right behind us.

'Nibbs, I've got a fight for you,' he said.

Nibbs's face lit up. 'Who?' he asked.

'Him over there.' Jimmy gestured to a big black man standing towards the back of the room.

Nibbs's face fell. 'Jimmy, that's fucking ———.' He named a well-known heavyweight fighter who had fought for the British title.

He was right, it was.

'He's about seventeen stone,' Nibbs told Jimmy. 'I'm only eleven.'

'It's four hundred quid, Nibbs.'

'No way.'

Nibbs turned around in disgust. He may have been strapped for cash, but not that strapped.

Five minutes later, Jimmy was back again. 'Six hundred, Nibbs.'

After another ten, it had risen to eight hundred pounds. Nibbs still didn't want to take the fight. I couldn't blame him.

The Big Man was desperate for a fight, more desperate even than Nibbs had been. He was supposed to have been matched with a local boy from the Bush, but he was a no-show. I watched him repeatedly going up to Jimmy the promoter and asking if he'd got him someone yet. I watched Jimmy shaking his head and the Big Man waving his hands around and becoming even more agitated. Nibbs could see it too. Jimmy tried once more with Nibbs, offering him another fifty. 'And you can keep the twenty I already gave you, Nibbs.'

Nibbs kept his head. 'Sorry, mate, I can't give an ex-pro six stone, can I?'

Then Jimmy jumped up in the ring.

'All right,' he shouted, trying to get some order. 'I've got a fight here if anyone wants it. Eight hundred pounds. You'll fight the Big Man here.'

I almost laughed out loud at Jimmy's nerve, but there was a big shout from over near the bar. A man was being encouraged by his mates to take the fight.

'Jimmy! He'll do it! Dave will do it.'

'You can take him, Dave son.'

Dave was persuaded. He pressed his way through people towards the ring. He was a tall man, and heavily built. His hair was razored low to his scalp. He had no kit with him, so he stripped down to his boxer shorts. Some gloves were found for him.

I asked Nibbs if he recognised Dave. Maybe he was a well-known scrapper.

'Never seen him before in my life, to be honest,' Nibbs answered.

I wondered if he had any idea that he was fighting a man who was once considered a prospect.

The Big Man entered the ring. He looked way past his prime. A large roll of fat hung over his shorts. His face was puffy. He was a bit like Larry Holmes in his later years.

The ref waved the fighters together. Dave jumped quickly into the middle of the ring, his gloves up peek-a-boo style. The Big Man pushed out a couple of jabs. The crowd around the ring hooted and hollered. Most were behind Dave. They admired a guy who figured a pasting was worth eight hundred quid. Most of the people there looked like they'd been hammered for a lot less from time to time.

The Big Man shoved Dave hard against the ropes and drew back his meaty right arm. He threw the shot. Dave bobbed at the knees as if he were a young Tyson. The punch sailed over his head. Dave fired his own shot into the air left vacant by the Big Man's punch. It landed flush on the jaw. The Big Man went down and stayed down. Dave danced for joy, jumping around from foot to foot, looking slightly absurd in his green stripy boxer shorts. The Big Man was hauled to his feet, and he staggered groggily towards his corner.

I turned around to Nibbs, whose face was stretched out as long as an ironing board.

'Well, fuck, I ain't ever seen nothing like that before in my life,' he said. 'I can't make that out. He's really gone downhill.'

I watched a creeping realisation cross Nibbs's battered, proud face.

'I could have done 'im. He's shot beyond belief. I could have hit him that hard.'

It was eight hundred quid down the drain for Nibbs.

CHAPTER SEVEN

BARE FISTS IN THE BACK ROOM

'When I think about him, I can't fucking describe what it's like
. . . It's a fucking feeling in the bottom of my belly and it goes
right up me. It actually makes me feel hot, sweaty. It's pure
fucking hatred, that's what it is, mate. Pure fucking hatred.
Believe this: if you said to me I could kill the cunt and never get
found out, then I would do it. It wouldn't bother me to kill
him. But as it is, I'll settle for kicking his fucking head off.
When I get in that room with him, it's all going to come out.
You'll have to pull me off him . . .'

And then Ray White laughed a humourless little laugh. The
thought of interrupting his bleak viciousness was almost
terrifying. He was a man whose violence was not channelled by
the ring. White was a streetfighter, a pub scrapper and a
hooligan. His brand of violence was nightmarish: boots,

knives, fists, heads, baseball bats, anything. I didn't know it, but I was about to bottom out, to drift away from boxing and into something altogether different, something ungoverned and with boundaries bordered only by darkness.

White was no fighter; he had no hint of the noble warrior about him. Beyond the bullshit and the braggadocio, boxers were among the most gentle men you could meet. They had an outlet for their aggression. It was held in sharp focus by the ropes and by the gym. It was spartan and coded and slightly heroic. White was none of those things. His short-circuited brain and kick-boxer's body were the very worst combination. He was like a madman with a gun, unconcerned with the consequences of what he did and what he was. His eyes were wild. They seemed to be open a touch too wide all the time. There was no human connection to be made with them and they offered no recognisable signals. If they were the window to his soul, then his soul was an empty quarter. If you held his gaze, he regarded it as a threat and a challenge for which his body seemed constantly primed. It twitched and tweaked. His quick-bitten fingers were never still. His words rattled out between them and his teeth, as the uneven white lines tried to chew the skin off the edges of his raw nails.

He had been playing pool in a pub near the Black Cap, but he'd decided he would come off the table to talk about Darren Lee. He wore an England football shirt and across his right forearm was a tattoo of a bulldog with the words 'British Bulldog' underneath. His other arm had a schoolyard inking across it, made with a pen and a needle or a compass point, spelling out 'JANE' in uneven letters. The knuckles on his hands were dotted with little white scars. The tendons in his neck tensed like piano wires when he spoke, and his large

Adam's apple bobbed up and down. His voice went through an alarming register, from a typically flat-vowelled estuary bark to a womanly shriek.

Someone walked into the bar.

'Ronnie, all right?' White asked loudly.

'Sound, mate.'

'You know that bird the other night? Fucked her!'

Ronnie just looked at him like he knew it was coming. White's mates laughed.

'Who was she, Ray?'

'This bird come in here,' White explained, turning back to me, 'giving it some, you know. Got fucking pissed, had a laugh and walked her home, and I give her one up against the wall down by the garages.'

* * *

The feud between Ray White and Darren Lee had gone on for so long, had undergone so many sly twists and false turns and had bled so much rotten, black blood, it was almost impossible for White to remember how or why it had started. Instead, he just spewed the story out freeform, fast and with an intensity that had his face inches from mine several times as he talked.

'He was all right for a while, right, this cunt Lee. Okay, I see him about and he sees me about and it's all right. He knows me, knows what I'm about, right? I first seen him when we was maybe fifteen. He's been around that long. I don't really like him, but so what? I ain't got nothing on him. I heard that he followed Chelsea, ran with them. Not the Headhunters, but some other crew. I'm fucking Charlton, right. If you're from round here, why are you fucking Chelsea? He was knocking off this bird that I used to go out with. Just this right silly slag. I'm in this club one Saturday, right, and in the cunt comes. So I'm like, "All right?" and he's, "All right, Ray?" So I just goes, "Tell Jackie Ray says hello . . ." Only in a joking way.

'He stops dead in his tracks, like, and goes, "What do you fucking mean by that?"

'So I'm thinking, is he having a pop, or what? Cos I'm not having it. So I'm like, "What do you think I mean?"

'"I don't know. Why don't you fucking tell me?"

'So it's all looking like it's going to go off. He won't back off. He's right in my face. Someone told me later that she was having his kid. I was on a bit of whizz. He's got a load of mates with him, but so do I. I'm up for sorting it out, but he walks away. He stays over the other side of the club, but there are plenty of verbals going on with his boys. We wait for them outside afterwards. He walks round the corner . . . I could fucking hear him coming. He never fucking shuts up. So he walks round the corner and I step out in front of him and do him, and it goes off with his mates. There's a bit of a punch-up. So I think that that's it, right? I've done him, and that's that. But I'm lying in bed one day, right, and the door nearly gets fucking knocked down, and it's the police. Fucking tipped off that I'm dealing. Fucking luckily, I had nothing in the house. So I get to hear that it's this Lee cunt that's put them on to me, so I goes out looking for him. I can't find him for a few weeks. Then his car gets done. Gets nicked and burned out. The fucking cops are round again.

'"Come on, Ray, we know it was you . . ."

'I'm like, "I never fucking done it." They couldn't pin it on me, though they think it's me cos I've found out he's given them the nod about me.'

'Was it you?' I asked him.

'Nah. I mean, I do know who done it. It was a mate of mine. He sorted it. He was at the club that night too. This was all, like, three years ago now, at least. I'm thinking that this cunt's full of it. I mean, what's all this fucking telling the coppers that I'm this, that and the other? I've done a stretch so they know about me, so it's easy to get them round my gaff. They'll put me in the frame for anything.

'Then I see Lee in the street one day. Up the market. "Come here," I go. He's like, "Fuck off." I said, "I'll fucking see you. Just say the word. We'll sort this out. Name a place and I'll be there." He just backs off.

'Nothing happens for a while, then my brother got mugged one night. Got his head kicked in. Three days in hospital, got to have his fucking teeth capped, the lot. I ain't got no proof, but I think that Lee done it. He's a low cunt.'

* * *

The feud died down for almost a year, and then, according to White, Darren Lee went to prison for three months for a minor offence. When he came out, he went looking for White, under the impression that White had somehow colluded in his arrest.

'That sums the silly cunt up, right? As if I'm going to fucking grass someone up! I'd be fucking done for it. The police are on one side and I'm on the fucking other. If I've got a problem with some cunt, I sort it. I don't go running off going, "Oh, please put this little cunt in prison cos I don't fucking like him." It ain't going to happen.'

White was angry even recounting the story, pissed off at what he saw as the lowest form of insult. The tension showed in his corded neck.

'About, like, two months ago, we're here drinking. In he comes with a load of mates. I'm ready for him there and then, even though he might have brought fuck knows what with him. But he puts out a challenge. I says, "Any time. We'll do it here."'

White looked up at the man behind the bar.

'He's locked us in before. We've had a few fights down here, over there.'

White nodded towards the back room.

'There ain't no problem. My mate had a fight in here against some fighter from Streatham. It was a good night. So it's set up for a few weeks, but then I hear it's off. Lee's mate says he's split his cheek open training. Had to be stitched up. So now it's Wednesday, but I don't reckon the cunt will show. He knows I can do him.'

White told me about the arrangements for the fight. It would be bare-fist and 'to the finish'. One or other would be carried out. There was no money involved; it was purely a grudge fight, a settling of differences.

'I'm right wound up for it,' White said. 'I've been back training. I used to go kick-boxing, but I gave it up. But I've been going back down for a few weeks, just getting sharp. I'm going to rip into him, hard and fast . . .'

I asked White if he'd ever fought bare-knuckle before.

'I always fight bare-knuckle, mate,' he grinned slyly.

'No, I mean like this. Prearranged?'

'Couple of times. I had this black geezer over in Brixton in a car park. That was for money. Short and sweet it was. Easy cash. And I had a bit of a tear-up when I was a kid, just before I went down. He was a bit of an older geezer, but he was fucking strong. We whacked each other a few times, but then we was just wrestling and we got pulled apart. There was another fight after, a big one, so they didn't want to see us pissing about.'

* * *

Others in the pub who knew Ray White had no doubt about who would win this bare-fist bust-up.

'You watch him. He's a bit of a headcase sometimes,' said White's friend Jim. 'I wouldn't touch him. He's not the bloke to be on the wrong side of. He's all right otherwise, though.'

That was unconvincing. Trying to get a handle on Ray White was impossible. He lived by a different code. He was unpredictable and extreme. When he was friendly, he was way over the top in his camaraderie. He had no concept of personal space. He'd sit a little too close, and sometimes he'd spray you with spittle, seemingly unknowingly. His mood could alter bewilderingly rapidly; it took him no time to tap into his anger. It was always about him, like a hard sheen. His response to most given situations involved violence of some kind or another. I wondered how he existed in the same streets as everyone else, lived the same life as everyone else, but somehow he did. His sociopathy was hidden from view, screened by the teeming mill of ordinary life around him. But the fight, I was sure, would strip that veneer away. Ray White would find himself exposed and bared by the contest, and we would see what he was.

* * *

The pub near the Black Cap was almost overrun by the time the hours until Wednesday night's fight had ticked away like those of a death sentence. The thought of White's brand of combat had no allure; in fact, it was the opposite. It was something to be missed, one to be avoided. But anyway, there I was, telling the big men on the door that I was here for 'Ray's party'. Any humour in that little password was unintentional. Ray White wasn't one for irony.

The landlord had kept the doors to the back room shut, and consequently the public bar was choked with lads, all boozing hard. White was closeted in the back room with three other men. He nodded me in.

'He's fucking coming,' he said, almost grunting. 'It's on. It's on. It's on . . .' A quiet mantra.

White paced around. He was slowly working himself into a condition of frenzy. His lean face could barely conceal the emotions that were corrupting it from underneath. His jaw bunched and the veins in his neck bulged as they filled with his boiling blood. White spit had congregated at the corners of his mouth. He looked like a dog in a cage, moving constantly to its boundaries, unpredictable only in the level of violence that may be meted out. On the only small table left in the bar stood glasses of whisky or brandy, I couldn't tell which, some empty, one still full. After a while, White flicked it down his neck.

'What's the time?'

'About half eight, Ray.'

'Half eight? He's got half an hour.'

I left White to it and stood outside in the early-evening dark. Across the road were some terraced houses. Through one of the bottom windows, I could see a woman watching television. A couple of kids crossed the road and went into the convenience store that stood on the opposing corner of a side road. Again there was a feeling of dislocation that such amoral rage could be expended so close by to this normality on an average Wednesday night. The feeling added to the awful bleakness of the fight. I was miles away from boxing, oceans away from it, unlicensed or not. There would be no sport here, nothing that resembled a testing of men. Mike Tyson had crossed this street during that hot desert night, but it had been a random schism. In this small, shabby pub, it was anything goes for White and Lee and their ferocious hatred. I wanted to walk away and just keep walking, but instead I turned around and went back in.

* * *

By the time Darren Lee showed up with twenty or so of his boys with him, the clock had stabbed past nine. The doormen stood in front of closed doors with their 'private party night' signs. We were moved into the bare back room. White remained in one corner with the same three men, and as people came through the door they nodded across to him and wished him well. Lee's men were the last to be let in. We stood three or four deep around the walls of the bar, leaving a fair-sized area

143

of ornate pub carpet free in the middle. Lee was surrounded on all sides by his team, and I was anxiously trying to get a look at him. In this company he didn't look too much like a tough nut. He was tall but not hugely robust. His skin was the colour of milky coffee and his features were almost elegantly patrician. He showed none of White's agitation. He looked cool, cool and ready, in fact. Perhaps he would bring some courage to the night.

By contrast, two men had kept hold of White almost paternally when Lee came in, seemingly anxious to stop him tilting across the room for an instant result. A second for Lee and a second for White stood in the centre of the room to keep some sort of order above the growing noise. Lee stepped out from his human cloak and stood a few feet behind his second, and then White came running out from behind his tiny corner table. A slow quiet came down, just for a few seconds, and then it was broken.

'Right, you cunt.' White was already moving forwards. His shouts of abuse seemed almost comical. 'Fucking . . .' White's voice tailed off. Both of the seconds pulled back quickly, aware that this was the most orderly start they were likely to get. Lee stood his ground and swung a wild, long punch as White closed him down. It landed somewhere on Ray White's shoulder. White whirled in a sickly shot of his own that smacked into Lee's head about halfway up his face. It made a noise like a hand slapping thick meat, heavy and dull, and there was no doubting its force and its effect.

The pair fell together and White tried to ram his head into Lee's, but made only partial contact. White freed his long right arm from Lee's grapple and threw a dizzying uppercut to the point of the chin. It was a concussive and conclusive punch and

Lee dropped to the floor under White's boots. White's eyes bulged open and he uttered a guttural 'Uuuuuurgh' – and then began to swing his boots into Lee, who had curled himself into a ball. White jumped into the air and landed hard on the curled-up form, digging down with the heel of his boot. Then his boys were on him, pulling him away. Even they looked alarmed at what might happen if White were left to his own vindictive devices. The heavy punches, the butt, the kicks, they had slaked none of his hatred for Lee. He reacted furiously to the attempts to drag him away, but the fire of his adrenaline had tired him quickly, and his mates were strong. He was yanked away, out of the back room.

Lee came around slowly, and got to his feet gingerly. His right eye was closing and he moved stiffly, his ribs singing under the assault of White's boots. His head stayed bowed as he took some consoling words.

* * *

In the end, the real darkness had been held at bay. The gangs of Lee and White showed none of the antagonism that White had claimed existed between them. The bubble of fear and loathing had popped easily. There was no stomach for any more fighting.

Lee looked tired. He wanted all of this to end, it seemed. The years of it weighed heavily on him in those moments. He walked slowly towards Ray White, who was in his usual corner of the public bar, nursing a table full of celebratory drink. Lee extended a hand towards Ray White and White took it without meeting Lee's eyes. The shake was perfunctory, and Lee left swiftly afterwards.

White got drunker as he relived the short seconds of the fight with his cronies. His view of the fight seemed entirely wrapped up in theirs. They backed him solidly every time he told them 'how hard I cracked him' and how, had he not been pulled away, 'I would have finished him right off'. They stroked him and his mood cheered. He had, he thought, settled the matter of Darren Lee and eight years of their feuding. Ray White had won.

I walked out into the unclean dusk, happy I would never have to see him again.

CHAPTER EIGHT

FINDING ROY

So, after a time, I went and found Roy Shaw. Many people
claimed to know where he was. He was in Bristol. He was in
the East End. He was in jail. He was punch-drunk and half
dead. He was gone, lost, a long shadow cast over a dying
endgame.

I had known about Roy since the beginning, since Mickey
Sullivan had lent me the video of his fights from the '70s,
when the game was raw to the point of being evil. John
Barnwell had fought him, and he still remembered his
strength. Mickey told me wide-eyed stories of his fights and he
worked on a door with a man who'd once faced him. Steve
The Hammer and Trev Foster had been linked to him. He was
more myth than man, a living link to the origins of modern
unlicensed fighting.

*   *   *

John and Mickey moved on from Danny's gym. The room under the Black Cap was no longer large enough to hold Danny's ambition. He was relocating the gym to a bigger place, with a new partner whom John and Mick disliked, so they went a few miles across town to a new gym above a pub. It was run by Brian Hills, a veteran trainer. Brian had had a lifetime in the game. On the gym walls were pictures going way back: Brian with Tony Sibson and Alan Minter, fight posters from bills in the 1950s, one at the Albert Hall on which all three of the Kray brothers appeared.

Boxers beyond number had passed through Brian's life. He had hair like Harpo Marx and small hands with swollen joints. His memory for fighters was encyclopaedic. He showed me a picture on his wall of himself standing with Joe Pyle. Brian credited Joe with starting organised unlicensed boxing in London. Joe was the manager of Roy Shaw.

I asked Brian if he knew where Roy Shaw was now.

'Roy Shaw?' he replied in his slow way. 'Nah. I was talking to one of my lads the other day, and he was asking about him. He must be in his sixties now. I don't think he's in London any more.'

John Barnwell remembered Shaw as 'a right hard bastard' – and that was some admission from John. He'd wrestled his way through his time in the ring with him. John had heard from a friend of his in Croydon that Shaw was punchy.

I tried many times, but no roads led to Roy Shaw. His most famous opponent, Lenny McLean, the self-appointed 'Guv'nor' and 'King of the Cobbles', had attempted to become an actor.

He had appeared in an ITV series called *The Knock* but had then been diagnosed with cancer, which he said was terminal.

One Sunday I opened the newspaper and saw a story about a new record by the musician Tricky. He had assembled a cast of characters from London's criminal underworld and got them to narrate some stories of their lives and crimes over a soundtrack that he'd written. It was called 'Products of their Environment'. There was a picture of the men on the record, lined up in two rows like a football team. And right there in the back row was Roy Shaw.

The caption described him as 'a bank robber'. I phoned the record company who looked after Tricky, but they seemed reluctant to give me a number. They thought that Roy was living in Bristol. Tricky had moved to New York and started his own branch of the label. After a month or so of calls and faxes, the American office called a pub where Roy was said to drink. A message was passed to him, and then I was told he was waiting for my call. He wasn't in Bristol at all, but near the M25 corridor in Essex.

*   *   *

His voice on the phone was not as I'd expected. It was softer, more eager to please. Roy was glad to talk. He gave me detailed directions on how to reach his house, and he promised to get all of his personal papers and photographs out so that we could look at them. He even offered to stand in his garden until I drove past so that I wouldn't miss his place. It was a large bungalow set behind some wrought-iron gates. On the drive was a gleaming red Bentley. I rang the doorbell, and there he was, a short man, not yet grey, in a blue T-shirt and training bottoms that contained a magnificent physique. His arms were like Popeye's. The last time I'd seen a middle-aged man with a build like Roy's it had been Ken Norton, who was in Vegas to watch a Tyson fight. Roy looked terrifically fit, and bright-eyed under his low brows. We went inside. Roy locked a large dog into a room by the front door. The bungalow was expensively and tastefully decorated. Roy told me he lived there alone.

'I've always been very lucky with property,' he said when he noticed me looking around. 'I make a lovely living from it.' I didn't doubt it. He showed off his home gymnasium and then led me into his dining-room, which overlooked the back lawn. On the dark-wood table, he'd spread out big bundles of newspaper cuttings and photographs. There was a large championship belt, which was inscribed 'Roy Shaw, Heavyweight Champion 1975–81'. Next to it was a copy of *Time Out* from 1981, with Roy on the cover, bare-chested and with his hands taped up ready for the gloves. The caption read, 'Roy "Pretty Boy" Shaw – Still the Hardest Man in London.'

Roy was a lively talker, a natural story-teller who kept jumping up to illustrate his stories with stagey staggers, hand-claps and punches. He told me about his property interests, which brought him a healthy income, and also how he'd come upon this bungalow, which was a long story of good luck on his part. He seemed to enjoy having some company. His weekly routine, which he never varied, meant that he went running every Monday, trained on Tuesday and Wednesday, went out on Wednesday night, rested Thursday, trained Friday and Saturday, went out Saturday night and rested Sunday. Things

that pleased him he liked to describe as 'lovely', and he pronounced the word lovingly, in his soft, breathy voice. He was
full of energy. The muscles in his big arms twitched and his
hands fidgeted. When I told him that he was supposed to be
punch-drunk he beamed, pleased that he was still the subject of
talk and rumour.

Roy made some tea. 'We're healthy in this house,' he said.
'Only powdered milk.' He served the tea in two fine china cups
with saucers.

I told Roy about John and Mickey and about the fights I'd
seen. He asked if I knew of Lenny McLean. Sure, I told him,
and I explained about the fight of theirs I'd seen on video.

'He'll tell you he done me twice, but he ain't. I beat him easy
the first time we had a row; it's in the paper there somewhere.'
Roy gestured to the pile of press cuttings. He was fond of
calling his fights 'rows'.

'I went and I fought this guy Ron Stander. Now he was
world class, an American fighter. I think he was number three
or four in the ratings.'

Ron Stander had been in the ring with Joe Frazier and
Earnie Shavers, and he had been world-ranked.

'Terry Downes got him over here. Now they think in
America, "Who the fuck's Roy Shaw?" You know, all our good
heavyweights go over there and we ain't in their class. So
Stander come over, and he was out every night with Terry
Downes, joking about, larking around, and Stander fell over
and he done his ribs. He never said nothing, and went in the
ring. So I was hitting him with some terrific punches on the
chin and he was going, "Go on, boy, go on. That's good . . . go
on." I couldn't believe it.'

Roy jumped up and demonstrated, peeking his chin out

from behind his raised fists to show how Stander had taken his best shots without a problem.

'I sunk one downstairs and he went "eeoooawhh". I've got it on the video somewhere. He fell out the ring cos of the injury to the ribs. But if he hadn't had that, no doubt he'd've ripped my head off. Me and McLean, we ain't even in that class.

'So then McLean said, "We'll fight again." So I said to my men, "All right, but who's going to back McLean?" I've already done him, I've done Ron Stander . . .'

Roy paused to sip his tea.

'When I was bashing McLean in the ring, he said to me, "Tell him to stop it, Roy. Tell him to stop it." So I put my hand in the air and the ref stopped it. I done Ron Stander, and I said, "Who's gonna put money on McLean now?"

'So I put money on McLean, and I doubled my purse. I was getting between twelve and fourteen grand a fight, so I just fell out the ring. Got about twenty-four grand.'

'So you fell over? It was a bent fight?'

'Yeah. I just fell out the ring. He hit me, I went down and he was jumping on me. I got up and I rang the bell, made the round short. He hit me again and I fell out the ring, so I let him have that one. Then we was going to have a return. I don't want to make excuses, but I used to take ginseng. I don't know if you know about ginseng, but it's supposed to be some good gear, and I used to take capsules. So I took one on the day of the fight and I felt lovely. In the East End there was a gym called Waggy Bennett's, and they had liquid ginseng. We had to drive past on the way to the fight, so I bought a bottle of that. When I'm in the car, I've drunk about three-quarters of the bottle, thinking that it's gonna buzz me up, make me like a terror. But it hasn't. I was walking into the ring. I was just like that . . .'

Roy stood up again and slumped down against the dining table. 'When I went in the ring I couldn't twig, but my woman could have knocked me out, let alone McLean. On the video, all the other fights I'm like this . . . alive . . .' He jumped up again and danced around, his arms twitching. 'On that one it's like I just got out of bed. That tells its own story. Anyway, it doesn't matter. We went to a pal of ours' benefit. I said to him, "McLean, all this talk about I beat you, you beat me . . . Let's get it on again."

'"Nah, Roy, I'm thirty-nine, forty now. I'm too old."

'I said, "Well, that's how old I was when I fought you and I beat you." But he wouldn't do it. A couple of years ago I challenged him face to face on the Garry Bushell TV show. I told Bushell the same story I'm telling you.'

The Garry Bushell show was a programme that went out about three o'clock in the morning, hosted by a man who wrote a television column for *The Sun*. Roy shook his head, still puzzled. 'I tried to get in touch with McLean and he'd moved. So I asked Billy Walker, you know, the fighter, and he had a word, but he said, "He won't fight you, Roy. He can't get fit."

'But that's the only mark I got on my record, and I know that in the first fight I stuck my chin out and he hit me and I didn't go down. If you can't punch then you can't learn to punch, so I know in my own heart I could have beaten him, and that hurts me.

'Before me, he wasn't even known, and since he beat me he's got where he is today. Mind you, he ain't all that. He's done a bit of television. I know he's ill, and I'm terribly sorry about that, but, you know, he tells fibs. He says he went to America and fought the hardest man in America, and he's fought this one and fought that one . . . When we was at the film studios, he said, "Oh, I might get Roy and have a scrap with him in a scrap metal yard." So I said, "Well, don't worry about it. I'll have you." I'd have loved it. I'd get meself fit. I go out running every morning over the forest here. It'd just take a little time to get back in the sparring, but I'm fit. I could get there in three or four weeks.'

All of this came out in a rush. Roy didn't seem to acknowledge his age. He was a fighting man and always would be, and he was ready to fight now.

'Do you mind me asking, Roy, how old you are?'

He stood up and grinned. He paused for a minute.

'I'm sixty-two,' he said, enunciating the figure as if he found it hard to believe himself. 'It's strange. I went on that Garry Bushell show to say all this to McLean, because he tells fibs. He says he's never been beat. There was a geezer who knocked McLean out twice, Cliff Field, he was a big, big boy. I wouldn't fight him because I knew he would have mullered me. I'm a middleweight, naturally. Well, Cliff Field knocked him out twice, Johnny Waldron knocked him out twice, I beat him once, that's five times. How can he give it all "I'm the guv'nor"? I went on the Garry Bushell show specially to say that, and I had all the names written down, but he shook me like you shook me. Garry Bushell said, "You're sixty now, aren't you, Roy?" and it all went out my head. It never come across . . .'

* * *

Roy began to talk about his life. It was terrifying, but fun to listen to. Like his stories about McLean, Roy rushed from this part to that in no particular order, recreating bits of dialogue and letting them lead him randomly from point to point. Every now and again he would apologise for racing ahead of himself. It was around the time that he told me that Britain's top prison psychiatrist had described him as 'the most dangerous and violent man he'd ever attempted to treat' that I realised I really liked Roy Shaw.

His life had been brutal, but his acceptance of its stark truths had left him stripped of pretence, stripped of anything but the reality of it. Roy's father had died when he was ten, shortly after he moved to Dagenham after fighting in the war. Roy had been evacuated to Wiltshire. After his father's death and the jolting move from country to city, his uncle provided a steadying influence and encouraged him to box. He began aged ten. A year later his uncle fixed him up with a fight at Aldgate in a fairground booth. He fought a lad of the same age who was one of the Smith family, a well-known brood of scrapping gypsies. Roy won the fight and three pounds. He could already punch, and box. Every time he went to the ring, he felt adrenaline surge up inside him, lending him power and ferocity. Roy was a wild kid, good-hearted but fiery. His energy and his temper began to dictate the pattern of his life.

'I went with my uncle to watch a police show once. I was about fifteen or sixteen, and he shot away and he said, "I got you a fight," and I was on the bill fighting a copper. I bashed him up. I ain't bumming my load, but I was pretty good. I was in the ABA finals and Mickey Duff, he said, "Roy Shaw is the most exciting fighter I've come across at this stage of my career," which was a bit of a gee. I was well pleased.'

Then Roy began his national service.

'Unbeknown to me, I had an anti-authority thing. I can't have anyone telling me what to do. I just used to rear up. And I was slung out the army and I got put in the nuthouse and everything. I was getting five court-martials at one stage. They sent me to Colchester, to the army prison, for nine months, and I come out of Colchester and they got me to Germany to get me out the way.

'The first night we went over to Germany, my mate says to me, "Come over, Roy." We went to this place in Minden called the Gorilla Club. It was this massive casino and dance hall, loads of birds in there. I was going up to them saying, "Wanna dance, darling?" They was getting a bit offish, cos I didn't realise you had to book your dances over there. The barman starts having a ruck at me and I'm having a ruck at him. They got the minders, and they was big. They said, "YOU GO!" My mate, he could have a bit of a row, but he wasn't that good. He was effing and c-ing.

'I said, "You wanna whack 'em?"

'"Yeah . . ."

'I got in position, all the weight on one side of my body, and I went BANG! – and he went down like a big tree.'

Roy swept his forearm downwards like a clock-hand to demonstrate. He grinned, savouring the feeling.

'I shouted, "Run!" There were two doors in front of us. My mate pushed his door, and it was open. I went to run through mine and it was closed, so I cut my hand. We get in this pub and I'm having a drink out the way, and all of a sudden the police come in.

'"Nah, we ain't been to the Gorilla," we said, and he said, "What's the blow on your hand?" I said, "Mechanic, you know . . ."' Roy gestured a man working underneath a car.

'"Come and wait outside for the MPs," he said.

'"Fuck that," I said, and we ran.

'He screams at us, "Stop, or I'll shoot!"

'I thought, "Cunt!" I mean, we won the war and all that. And he went "bang" and my mate was hanging on the back of the bullet. We was puffing round the corner and this copper came with a big .45, so we said, "All right . . ."'

Roy raised his hands in surrender and grinned. 'They handed us over to the British army and they put me on this "confined to barracks", where you wasn't allowed out of the army camp. It all went off there. I done a couple of guards. Some Americans came and stayed there. They was always chatting up these lovely birds and they had plenty of money, and so I done a couple of them and nicked their money. The army police nicked me, but not before I put the money down my trousers. They put three of us in the back of the cells. In front of us there was a great big room where all the guards went to sleep. They was a bit scared of us in there, so I said, "Let us all in later, so we can have a chat." They let us all into this big room. And all these kids were coming by and passing out, because you had to go through the guard room to go off duty.

'They had a big axe and a big crowbar on the wall. So a geezer passed the crowbar and I put it down my trousers. We banged on the door and said, "Come on, we wanna go back to our cells now." They put us back and I got the crowbar and I ripped my windows out, and I went along to the other cell and I ripped his windows out, so there's two of us. We whacked a sergeant and got away, took off down the autobahn. Anyway, we ended up at this brothel. I had this money I'd stolen, and the bird was saying I was taking too long, so I said, "Well, give us my money back." She wouldn't, so again, they had minders, and we done the minders.

'When they took me to the CO, he said, "I've had enough of you, Shaw. We don't need scum like you in the army." He was having a right go, so I jumped over the desk and whacked him. Even one of the RPs, he said, "Roy, you're getting in plenty of trouble."

'"You don't have to tell me."

'"Tell 'em you hear voices, Roy. Tell 'em you hear voices or you're gonna go away." So I went in. I'd superficially cut my wrists. Then I was supposed to tell the CO about the voices, but I bottled it. I saw the RP outside.

'"Did you tell him?" he asked.

'"No," I replied.

'"Oh, doctor," he said. "Shaw'd like a word with you." I went back in. I had a pal of mine called John and I knew this bird called Jean, so I told him that John kept telling me to do things and Jean kept trying to stop me. So they took me to this hospital place, scrubbed all my charges and slung me out the army.'

* * *

'I got to borstal, and in the borstal they had these blokes called the daddies. We was in this place called Usk. There was a closed prison and they had another part that was open. This place was called the jug. And the night I got there, they was having a boxing show, so I said I'd have a go, and I got the daddy of the jug. I just sparred and I went, "bing" – it wasn't even a hard punch – and they're all going, "What are you doing?"

'The guv'nor of the camp said, "I'll have it with you." So I got in there and I did him, and I'd done the two daddies in the first night, so I was respected in the borstal straightaway. I was on the party chopping down trees, which was nice, kept me nice and fit. And then I escaped for three months, and that's when I went with Mickey Duff. I boxed under the name Roy West. That's when it all started with the pro. I had ten fights with Mickey Duff and won them all, six by knockout. Not a bad record, but then I was captured.

'When I come out the borstal I tried to get my licence back, but unbeknown to me – I dunno if you know – all the board of control was QCs and magistrates and everything. They said, "Where have you been for the last three years?" and I said I'd been working all over the place, plastering and that, but they all knew I'd been in prison. Anyway, they knocked my licence back. So I went robbing banks and I got fifteen years.'

* * *

Roy served all of those fifteen years without remission. The story of his time in prison, which he told with humour, was far more harrowing when it was played back on my tape recorder, without his little smiles and jumps and gestures to ease it. I sat in the dark listening to it. Roy's voice was soft, then loud; soft then loud; singing sad songs of fifteen years when he lived close to madness and death.

'Someone told me that if you go to this Grenden Underwood, you can have visits where you can go in a room with your wife. It's a psychiatric prison. So to get there, as soon as the screws said anything, I boshed them, so they thought I was a nut,' Roy said. 'And the governor there seemed quite nice; he was helping me along. I had a visit from my wife, and took some flowers. She's a bit hot-headed, so we had a row and she threw the flowers at me. I went back to the wing, doing my nut. I was pushing the screws back and I rang the bell. If you ring the bell in prison it means there's a real emergency, and they come running from all over. I ripped this lump of iron off the washing-up table and I was going, "Come on," and they wouldn't. The governor came in and said, "Put that down, Roy." So I did. He said, "I know you've had trouble with your visit. I've talked with the matron and you can have a visit with your wife in my room." So they put us in the office. He said, "I'll be outside. Just give us a knock when you've finished." So as soon as he went, up with her skirt and we had a little bit of bunkies in the office.

'I was getting in bits of trouble and they was a bit scared of me. They had all these sex cases. We had to do this group therapy. You had to say if you had a problem, and people would try to help you over it. Anyhow, this bloke says, "I'd like to get this off my chest. I had a relationship with a dog."

'I said, "What sort of dog was it?"

'He said, "Alsatian."

'So I replied, "Oh, good-looking dog."

'So the doctor goes, "Shaw!" and I had to go out of there. Anyway, this Dr Unwin, the top psychiatrist, he took me in his office, and he told me that if you got to Broadmoor, they'd even send you home for weekends. So I thought, "I've got to try for Broadmoor."

'"Roy," he said. "You've lost all your remission, and if you do any more, you're going to get more on your sentence and you're never going to get out. I want you to have a word with your wife and think about Broadmoor." So I went there.

'They said I was a psychopath, but there was loads of kids in there like me. In Broadmoor there was a wing called Block Seven, and most of the kids in there had nothing wrong with them. It was just the anti-authority thing. The screws at other nicks would go, "Come on, Shaw, get in your cell." And there'd be trouble. But in Broadmoor it was, "Roy, are you ready?" It was the same thing, only the words were nicer. Loads of geezers were coming from the prisons and going to Broadmoor and getting in no trouble. So they had a big wing of them.

'There was a couple of nuts in there. I had my breakfast one morning, and went to the toilets. And they had three stalls with gaps under the doors. So I'm sitting there having a pony, and the door opens. I says, "Can't you fucking see I'm in here?" and the bloke went, "Oh," and walked off. I said, "Shut the fucking door," and he started beating me up, while I was sitting on the toilet. So I bashed him. The doctor said I went over the top on him, but I never did. When a geezer went down, that was it. I stopped.

'They called me down, and they said I went over the top and I had to go to Block Six. All the screws were waiting to take me over there. I had a right row, fractured the chief's cheekbone, done a couple of the others. They took me over there, opened the door and injected me. I was like a sack of shit, doped up. One of the cleaners come round and said, "Roy, Scotty's on." He was one of the screws who took me over there, a little squashed-nose geezer. He had my dinner. I'll always remember it was herrings. I pushed it in his face, still all doped up, then I put my head in his face, smashed all his face. Then they all come in, but I was like a sack of shit. And they kept me in there all doped up. They can do that till you're dead.

'My pal Joey Pyle and his boys, they were running the West End. They had Joe Louis over to open this casino, and they said to him, "Would you go up and see Roy, and show some of the films of your fights?" So we had all Broadmoor in this big hall, and Joe Louis showing all these films. And he said, "Thanks for looking, but now I want to have a visit with Roy." That set me on a bit of a pedestal. Then, about three months later, we done the same thing with Terry Downes. Another one was Jimmy Savile. He come in and saw me. So I was on a bit of a pedestal.

'Anyway, what they did was they got the cheese, the chief of Broadmoor, and took him up the Astor Club, fitted him up with a hostess, and he made friends with this old boy, a lovely, lovely man called Sulky. One night I was down in the dungeon because I kept doing the screws. No one goes down there at night; they're complete and utter nuts down there. At about ten o'clock at night, there's a knock on the door and it's Sulky. I said, "What's the matter?" The screw says, "You got five minutes." Sulky says, "Roy, Roy, you gotta stop doing the screws or they're going to kill you, Roy. Tell the doctor you ain't gonna do it."

'So I shook his hand, and said, "Don't worry about it." In the morning, I saw the doctor. I said, "This vendetta I got against the screws, I think it's a bit silly. All I want to do is do my time and get out."

'"Glad to hear that, Roy. Go back to your cell, and see how it goes."

'So the next morning, there's one of the screws I was going to do. "Morning," I went. He went, "Morning," and when I never attacked them they put me out there on to the main wing. And they made me a parole patient. I was walking all round, working in the gardens. It was like a holiday camp.'

* * *

'One of the charge nurses in Broadmoor was an old-time fighter, so we got on pretty well together. One day I said to him, "Can I have a look at my records?" So he put me in a cell and let me read through them. Well, I was in the right place to read them. They exaggerate everything: "Oh, he nearly killed me"; "If it wasn't for my companion he would have killed me". Every time I'd done the screws they were really, really stronging it. Then when I went to Grenden Underwood and I met that Dr Unwin, I thought he was real good to me. So I was reading this thing, and it had in red letters: "Roy Shaw is the most powerful and dangerous man I've ever attempted to treat." Well, fuck me. I said to the nurse, "What chance have I got of getting out now?" That was that so-called nice doctor.

'I must have been a powerhouse, though. I was in the powerlifting team. There were three of us, and Reggie Kray was one of them. I was up to sixteen stone. We were shifting some heavy, heavy weights. Six hundred pounds we were dead-lifting; some heavy, heavy weights we were slinging about. All you got in the nick was a little mirror that you shaved with. I didn't know. Then I was moved from one nick to another, and in the reception they had a full-length mirror. I got a look at myself and I couldn't believe it. I was like a little oxo cube. I was too short to be sixteen stone. Fuck me. When I think to myself now, the weights we were slinging about, I must have been a powerhouse. At the end of my sentence, they kept moving me around, three months here, three months there, solitary confinement all the time. I said to the govenor of the last place, "Do you want any trouble?"

'"What?"

'"Do you want any trouble down there in the chokey?"

'"No."

'"Then give us some dumbbells in my cell, or I'll build up such a tremendous amount of energy I'll end up doing a screw."

'So he went, "All right." So I sealed the dumbbells up. Had to get a weight that I could do all my workout with. So I had eighty-pound dumbbells. Now that's quite a weight. I ain't bumming myself out, but I got warmed up with them. How can you get warmed up with eighty-pound dumbbells? I must have been a powerhouse.'

* * *

'When I was in Parkhurst, we were down on the football ground. My mate's playing football, and he's having a bit of a ruck with this bloke. So he calls me over, and I says, "Shall we do him? Wait till we get to the top of the stairs, then we'll do him."

'So we get to the top of the stairs and we do him, and he falls down. Bang! I says to my mate, "Go on, fuck off, fuck off." I dragged him up, and it must have been the wind in him. He went "ooooh" and I thought he was waking up, so I hit him again.

'I used to get cobs with Gorgonzola cheese as my treat then, and I was eating those when the screw comes into my cell and says, "Can you let us know what happened on Saturday after the football?"

'"Nothing. I came back up here and banged myself up. How is he, the geezer?"

'"He's dead."

'I thought, "Fuck me." Yeah, so we got took out for murder, me and my pal. We had the case at Parkhurst. There were two poofs, I think it was, giving evidence against us. So they come in and I'm looking at them. One said, "We were coming in from the football pitch. Shaw and Coster were behind me, and Brown was behind . . ." That was the name of the dead kid, Brown.

'I jumped up and I said, "Then what did you see? Tell the truth."'

Roy leapt to his feet and gripped the sides of the dining table like it was a dock. He was shouting to demonstrate what he had done.

'The witness says, "Then Brown was at the bottom of the stairs and Shaw was helping him up."

'So my solicitor says, "Helping him up?"

'The magistrate says, "Any more of that and you'll be back in the cells, Shaw."

'My pal goes, "Keep it up, Roy."

'So the next one comes in, and he's saying about how he's at the top of the stairs, and I go, "Then tell the fucking truth! You didn't see nothing."

'He said he didn't see anything, and that was it. My brief said there's no case to answer. My mate didn't have a brief. He went through with the case and got six months to run concurrently. And that was it. Just a fight. Terrible accident.

Young kid lost his life. It is tragic, and I ain't proud of it. It's just one of the things that happened, but not many people get took out for murder in prison and get away with it.

'Because of all that they put me in Gartree. I was in the gym with the two PTIs, working out, couldn't be happier. They were like friends in the end. No one bothered me or nothing. And one day we were having our tea and the whistle goes, and there's these kids trying to cut the wire and get out. And the screws were hitting them with sticks when one of them gets a hammer out of a workman's bag and smashes someone over the head. And it went off. Fuck me, they tore everything apart. So I got a book, shoved it in the door – big, heavy, cell door – and popped it off. We were banging open the cell doors of the nonces and doing them. On the wing there was all this thick glass, and behind it was the strong room, and Frankie Fraser was in there. So I'm bashing it and smashed a big hole. I said, "Come on, Frank, come out with us."

'He said, "No, you'll get into trouble."

'So we put him down some coffee, and he was walking up and down, going, "Never been known before, coffee in the strong box . . ."

'Anyway, it didn't last long. A couple of days and we were all back in our cells. They smashed all the windows out – fucking freezing, it was.'

* * *

'I was coming to the end of my sentence and they kept moving me, three months here, three months there. I was just wasting

it away. I ended up in Durham. Who should be the commis-
sioner, but the old governor of Parkhurst. So we sat there
having a chat. I said, "I dunno what's happening. I've done
nothing and I'm not being treated right."

'"All right, Roy, leave it with me," he said. So a few weeks
later I was moved to Long Larton, and there was a bit of
friction going on. They wanted to get a new feeling in the
prison, so they had the screws calling you by your first name.

'"So, Roy . . ." they'd say.

'"I'm not fucking Roy. I'm Shaw to you," I'd reply.

'There was a bit of friction. I didn't want to be their mate.
The governer walked around in this fireman's hat, a cheese
cutter, looked like a div. But he called me up one day, and he
said, "Shaw, I'm not supposed to tell you this, but you're
fucking it up . . ."

'"What?"

'"You're getting parole in six weeks."

'I thought, "What?" They were gonna let me out! So that
was the end. Twenty-one prisons I was in. That's quite some
number. I was the only one I know about who's gone right
through a door. They were exceptional things, what I done.'

* * *

When Roy got out of jail, he was nearly forty. He had two
children who had grown up without him, but he said that he
didn't feel old. 'Frankie Fraser said to me that he thought time
in prison kept you young. The world keeps moving, but you
stop. If you meet him now, he's like a kid, and I'm a bit the same.

'The only way I knew how to get money was robbing banks. I had this big plot of land and I needed all the building materials to build a house, but by the grace of God, Ronnie Smith come along and he said, "Come to Barnet Fair, Roy. You can earn a few quid fighting the Pikeys." So I said, "All right." There's probably two or three grand in it; they chuck you a chunk of the dough. So I had a few fights up there. Let's be fair; they're only Pikeys, and I was a professional fighter. I know how to punch, know how to move about. They're only streetfighters. And Donny The Bull was there. He was the King of the Gypsies. And I knew him, I was in prison with him. They said, "Do you wanna fight him?" and I said, "Yeah." And that's when it all started. It took off, and then we started earning good money. What we done was, we started the unlicensed fights.'

Roy's fight with Donny 'The Bull' Adams was a grudge match. They had planned to hold it bare-fist in the traditional style; the police were alerted. Roy pulled out some yellowing pages from *The Sun* and the *Evening Standard* which catalogued their attempts to fight bare-fist, and also the taunting of Donny The Bull. He called Roy 'a great useless pudding', which, as pre-fight insults go, was hardly in the Ali class. Neither was his fighting. When the fight went ahead, at a nightclub, with gloves, Roy ended the contest with the first punch – although he admitted he'd handed out some 'afters' because he had objected to The Bull's pre-fight attitude.

Roy was looked after by Joe Pyle, the man who had taken Joe Louis to Broadmoor to meet him, and also Alex Steen, a jovial chancer who wore sunglasses even in the gym. Roy's brutal style, his hard-man image and his fearlessness packed venues all around London. His talent for violence, hidden for so long behind prison walls, was on public display.

The video that Mickey Sullivan gave me bore testimony to Roy's love of fighting. Even in his third, losing bout with McLean, he revelled in the fight, in hitting and being hit. He was like Billy Heaney writ large, a man apart, a progeny of violence.

'There wasn't a hard fight there. They were just villains with a reputation who could have a row. But they couldn't really. Being a professional boxer puts me three steps ahead of any of them. How to move, how to pace myself. The three rounds I had with McLean, they weren't hard because I was just walking through him, whacking him. But then again I ain't saying I'm a bit special.

'I went to see a geezer called Starbuck. He had a reputation over south London; he had about fourteen knockouts. He wasn't all that impressive, so I made a comeback and I fought him and he went in the first round. He was such a nice bloke, though. He was flat out; his nose was in the canvas. I caught him with a nice one. His wife got in the ring, and she stepped over him and shook my hand. Ain't that lovely? I met him afterwards and I asked, "You get any money out of it?" And he said, "Yeah, I got the most I ever got out of a fight." And I said, "Well, that's what it's all about." I was so pleased for him that he got his dough, and I got my dough, and after that I knocked it on the head. I was having luck with my property and I didn't need it.'

* * *

Someone came to the door and handed Roy a roll of cash. 'I'll just put this away,' he said, and wandered off. When he returned, he said that he had more money than he could spend.

'What can you do? I go away on holiday, come back, go away on holiday, come back. I ain't got nothing else to spend it on. All I'd like is a nice lady to share it with. I've had plenty of birds back here partying and that, but it ain't the same. It's a bit empty.'

Empty was right. The opaque cruelty of Roy's life had deprived him of something. He had lived with violence for so long, he had been immunised against it. He probably didn't realise how threatening he was, how his eyes could throw out implacable promises of violence, even in fun. His openness and honesty made him vulnerable. Like Tyson, his person was obscured by the image of him, by his myth. He could never be sure who was interested in him for who he was and who was just interested for what he'd been. He was not remorseful in any conventional sense. He had accepted the attritional nature of his life, but the sadness hung around him like a shadow all the same. Roy's days had been so hard that he had lost the need for tenderness. Maybe that was where the sadness lay, where the remorse would come. His house was beautiful and neat, but it smelled of his sweat and effort, and of his dogs. Roy needed someone, and his need was almost heartbreaking.

* * *

He hadn't had a fight for years, he said. Then the other week he'd been in a nightclub on one of his Saturday nights out.

'This bloke came up to me and said, "Roy, can you go and

stand with that girl over there? Her boyfriend's beat her up and raped her. She's got an order against him to keep him away, but he's in the club." So I went over. She was a lovely little girl. She told me what had happened, and showed me him. He was a big, lairy geezer, all long arms. Thought he was a bit special. He went in the toilets and I went in after him. There were all these people in there, and I was thinking, "Fuck off, fuck off." Then they did. So I put my hanky in my hand . . .'

Roy jumped up from his seat. He pulled a handkerchief from his pocket and demonstrated how he wrapped it in his right fist to protect his knuckles. Then he got in his 'position', standing crouched, with his left leg leading.

'I said, "Hit any more women lately, cunt?"'

'"I don't want that, Roy," he said. "I ain't got a fight with you."

'"Yes you have, cunt," I said, and I went, "BANG!" Down he went.

'I felt all the adrenaline rushing up from my stomach. It was like a force. That's where my power comes from. It just surges through me. I felt it, and it was just like the old days again.'

CHAPTER NINE

SLOW RIVER ROLLING

After Ray White and Roy Shaw, things seemed bleak for a while. Events had hit a downturn all the way across boxing, licensed and unlicensed. The inspiration of lives like John's and Mickey's and Billy Heaney's – hard lives played out against the cut of things – had been tempered by more darkness than I could have imagined. There had always been courage in the gyms, and many of the best human qualities on display, but they felt distant. Even the pro boxing game was under withering attack. The fallout from Mike Tyson's ignominious Vegas nightmare had opened both him and the sport up to ridicule. The heavyweight game had become a freak show, with breakdowns in the ring, disqualifications, farces, positive hepatitis tests, court cases, pay-per-view and sundry manias casting a veil across the sport of Ali and Marciano, Louis and

Frazier. The brightest star in the British ring, Naseem Hamed, had more people tuning in on the off chance of seeing him defeated because of his excess of arrogance than he had fans in awe of his incendiary skills.

The unlicensed game had shown all of its sides, and after the Billy Heaney scrap with Steve The Hammer they had all been harsh and hard to swallow in their different ways. In the midst of it, I went to Birmingham to write a newspaper piece about a trainer who ran a stable of willing pros noted for their lack of winning pedigree. They were nicknamed 'Losers Limited'. With the unlicensed so grim, I was expecting a little more bleakness, another dash of salt in the wound.

Birmingham didn't look like it would do me any favours, or anyone else. The gym I was looking for was perched above the Aston Expressway, on the edge of the ugly knot of motorways that ran towards the city's outskirts. The building was huge and hollow and cold, with concrete walls and a security guard in a cage. I climbed the stairs, looking for Nobby Nobbs.

* * *

The sign over the gym door read 'Norman Nobbs: Manager and Trainer of Champions'.

'It's true an' all,' said its proprietor, as he sat back in his old chair to watch two of his boys have a move around in the ring. Norman Nobbs, known universally as Nobby, was a tall man, slightly stooped, with a bald head and a long and delicate nose. He had several teeth missing and he was wearing an old cardigan that looked as if it had seen almost as many rounds as its owner. But he had clear, sharp eyes, smooth skin and good grooming.

'Now, see this lad here,' he said, after offering a warm welcome and a mug of weak tea. 'Been with me a couple of months. He moves worse than Douglas Bader. He had one fight in the amateurs. Stevie Wonder beat him on points. But I'll have him fighting soon.'

The wisecracks were Nobby Nobbs's stock in trade. They had been for thirty years, as had the journeyman pros who would fight anyone, anywhere, anytime – the Martini kids.

Fame of sorts has come late for him, after almost a lifetime in the game. Central Television made a documentary about him. It was called *Losers Limited*. Then, in the hurtful court case between Steve Collins and the promoter Barry Hearn, which had been heard in Ireland, Hearn told the court of Paul Wesley, one of Collins's opponents: 'He comes from the stable of Nobby Nobbs, who runs a stable of losers, and he has the busiest stable in the country. Whenever you need a loser, you get Nobby Nobbs.'

Nobby didn't mind the Losers Limited label; in fact, he thought it up. He didn't like Hearn's comments to the court, though, because Wesley had taken the Collins fight at two weeks' notice and had got beaten only on points. In his next fight, Collins took a version of the world super-middleweight title from Chris Eubank.

'If they treat you like a fool, act like one. Fuck 'em,' Nobby said, with a twinkle. 'But I ain't no fool. My fighters walk in and walk out. They ain't signed to no promoters, so they have to go the long route. They get bad decisions. I tell them, "Fuck it. You got your money. Forget about it. On to the next one."'

Nobby's phone was rarely silent. Promoters from all around

the country called him when they hit trouble, because Nobby's fighters could grab their kit and bail them out, all for a few hundred quid. He joked that the parachutist who interrupted the second Holyfield-Bowe fight was one of his, taking the contest at short notice.

On one famous occasion, the durable featherweight Pete Buckley was at home settling down for the night when Nobby arrived, sounding his car horn.

' "Can you fight in London? We're leaving now," I said,' grinned Nobby. 'All he's done is chucked his bag out the window, jumped in the van – hasn't known who he's fighting or how much he's getting – fought, done his job and come back.'

The self-deprecating one-liners had seen Nobby through a hard life, along with his large, lean frame and a big and boundless heart. He was born in Kingstanding, the part of Birmingham's rough inner city where he still lived. He was raised by his grandparents and left school at fourteen for a job on the market and £4 a week. After twenty years as a doorman, he was working back on the markets again, getting up at 3 a.m. six days a week to drive a van that distributed fruit and veg.

Nobby and his mate first walked into a gym to try their luck. 'I was crap, he was good, so I started training him. I got my first gym and that was it.'

His current place bore an eloquent testimony to his success. It was a large, high-walled and cold room, but two and a half of the four walls were covered from floor to ceiling in show posters. Nobby had fighters on every bill, hundreds and hundreds of them.

I walked around reading them. There were a few yellowing press cuttings, too, in amongst them. Clement Freud had once written about Nobby when Nobbs helped out Carl 'The Truth'

Williams when he came to Birmingham to fight Frank Bruno. Naturally, 'The Truth' had his lights turned out that night.

Nobby's philosophy was a simple one: 'The name of the game is to walk in and walk out. Anyone could get knocked out. You could. Walk in and walk out. I tell 'em, fuck skipping and exercises, get in.' His lessons were as simple as a referee's last instructions: 'Defend yourself at all times and come out fighting.'

Nobby had never had a 'Bomber' Graham walk through his door, or a Naseem Hamed, like his friend Brendan Ingle had. Instead, he got streams of kids who had heard about his gym on the street and had found an oasis, away from the slippery mix of drugs and crime that characterised the backstreets surrounding the Expressway. Some would slide back, but plenty became hard-working, durable pros who held down day jobs and fought anywhere at the drop of a hat, because Nobby asked them to.

'I teach 'em it ain't all satin gowns and bright lights,' he told me ruefully.

Nobby sat on a stool over by one of the heavy bags with his back to the door. When it clattered open, as it began to do regularly as the working day ended and the fighters came in to train, he'd look at me sitting opposite and say, 'Black or white?' I would tell him whether the man coming in to train was black or white and Nobby would look up at the clock and name him.

The door clattered again.

'Black or white?'

'White.'

'Tony Hanna.'

The boxer laughed. It was obviously one of Nobby's favourite tricks.

'Right on, Nobby,' Tony said.

*   *   *

Tony Hanna was a typical Nobby Nobbs fighter, a fast, lissom flyweight who had been in with Mickey Cantwell three times. He worked at a recycling plant and the gym kept him straight. His brother John and his mates first took him to Nobby 'so they could slap round the little brother, I think . . . and I kept coming'.

Tony Hanna's brother was dead, killed during a police chase, and many of his mates still lived in the shade of drugs and the black economy.

'Nobby's always there,' he told me after he'd run through his workout. 'You know you can always knock on his door, day or night, and you'll get a cup of tea and some help with your problems. He'll give you a tenner or a twenty if you're broke.'

Nobby's door wasn't open just to boxers. The day prior to our meeting, a kid had gone round to Nobby in tears because his heroin habit was raging well out of his control. He couldn't kick it, and he couldn't tell his mother because he was afraid of what the knowledge might do to her. By the time Nobby had finished with him, he walked down the road and into a clinic.

'Everyone knows Nobby round here,' Hanna affirmed. 'He could have anything he wanted. People would do anything for him.'

Nobby had watched while the city he had known all his life fell apart.

'I've been in court more times than Boris Becker, bailing people out. The judge knows me by name. Every year, the government puts up beer and fags; now look at it . . .'

He illustrated his point by calling across the gym to a couple of fighters to ask them what the most valuable goods on the black market in Birmingham were. 'Drink,' came the answer, 'or fags.' Nobby shrugged, his point proven.

'You can get a bag of heroin for a tenner. The kids on it would sell your eyeballs to get it. Stick a knife in you.'

Nobby Nobbs and his gym gave fighters perspective. They could lose a boxing match and live a little better because of it. When abolitionists talk about the fatalities in boxing, they fail to weigh against them the lives that it has saved. And when Barry Hearn called Nobby Nobbs a provider of losers, he had failed to understand that everyone in his gym has already won.

Nobby looked around the room. It cost him £170 a month to rent it, and he wouldn't charge any fighter for training there.

'This is my domain here,' he nodded, taking in each of the four walls and the high ceiling. 'It's a haven for us. Anyone can call me a cunt except my fighters. I'm not jealous of Frank Warren or Brendan Ingle. Good luck to them. You make your own luck. I just wish I could make enough from this so I didn't have to work on the market any more.'

And that one day a new Naseem Hamed would walk in off the streets, up the cold stairs and through the door with its proud sign: Trainer of Champions.

* * *

The shock and blood of the MGM ringside soon dissipated, and the fallout from 'Mike's Bite Night' saw the Baddest Man on the Planet slip towards ridicule. Jay Leno, David Letterman and Bob Monkhouse rolled up their television audiences with their 'Don't ask Mike for dinner' routines. The journalists and commentators wrote themselves to a righteous pitch. He should never fight again – but the consensus was that he would, in a year, when he would become eligible to reapply for his licence to box. The dollars would dictate it.

Mike Tyson himself had vanished like vapour into the distant Nevada mountains. He still hung over the sport, a sharp reminder of its underbelly, of its proximity to the edge. His despair was not hard to imagine. It seemed that the bad end that he had always alluded to, that he had always half-expected to come to him, had moved closer now that the ring was again denied to him. In an eloquent conversation in 1996 with the writer Donald McRae for his book *Dark Trade: Lost in Boxing*, Tyson's co-manager John Horne had said, 'It's very difficult for Mike to talk about his life five years from now. I'll be honest, there are days when Mike just does not believe he is still going to be here five years from now. He's not sure how much time is left for him. He does not know what life might throw at him next.' Well, now he knew.

Tyson faced the first black days of his disgrace alone with his family. He broke his silence when he gave a rare television interview to the ESPN and Sky networks in the autumn of 1997. He appeared relaxed and even-tempered before the cameras, and even allowed a team to film him at his Ohio home with his wife, Monica Turner, and their children. 'He is,' his wife said, 'a wonderful father.' Tyson just grinned his gold-toothed grin as his daughters crawled over him. He opened up freely about his attack on Holyfield. 'I just lost my mind out there,' he said gently, explaining that the fear that the butt which had opened up his eye would cost him his shot at regaining the title, and the looming dread that he may be beaten again, had caused his brain to short-circuit. He gave only one hint of his more customary menace, when he was asked what he thought of the people who said he was a coward who should never be allowed back to the ring.

'I can't say,' Tyson noted quietly, nodding at the camera.

'Yes you can, Mike, go ahead.'

'Nah, I can't say, man.'

'Go on, Mike, say what you think.'

'Fuck them,' he hissed slowly, lifting his chin. And then right into the camera: 'Fuck them . . .'

The Baddest Man was offered the chance to cash in on his notoriety by the World Wrestling Federation, who gave him $4 million for fifteen minutes of his time to referee one of their cartoonish 'sports entertainment' pay-per-view events. Iron Mike obviously felt that the predictable jibes that followed the announcement of his new job were worth enduring for the small fortune that was about to drop into his pocket. He played along gamely, glowering his way through the bout and even joining in the fun by shoving one competitor across the ring in a fit of mock rage.

The more serious business was being played out away from the cameras, though. With two months left before his bid for reinstatement, Mike Tyson made a significant move towards the control of his destiny, whatever it might be. He announced a $100 million lawsuit against Don King pertaining to a loss of earnings, and simultaneously broke up Team Tyson, cutting off the payroll to John Horne, Rory Holloway, Richie Giachetti and their staff. Don King had made and lost Tyson one fortune. He wasn't about to see him repeat the trick. Team Tyson were left wondering what to do about the Team Tyson tattoos they had all proudly displayed on their forearms at The Sound and the Fury. 'It's a family affair,' the fancy script had boasted. Well, Daddy had just stopped their pocket money.

Tyson moved quickly to appoint a new adviser, the veteran Shelly Finkel, and announced that he was open to bids from promoters on a fight-by-fight basis. At the same time, he indicated his intention to reapply for his licence to box, not in Nevada, but closer to his Catskill home in Atlantic City. While the Nevada State Athletic Commission made affronted noises that only they could relicence Tyson, the move made good sense given Don King's shadowy influence in Las Vegas. Aside from being Tyson's spiritual boxing home, packed with the ghosts of his rise to greatness in the 1980s, Atlantic City had one other huge advantage for Mike. Don King had no licence to promote there.

Boxing *realpolitik* continued to hiss and whirr behind the scenes. Involvement with Mike Tyson and Don King had been disastrous for the MGM Grand Hotel. Along with the giant site fee they had lured the pair with, the terms of their agreement meant that Don King could claim vast stock options when the contract terminated in September 1997. When King cut the MGM deal in 1995, he secured from the hotel a 'no-interest loan' of $15 million to allow him to purchase around 600,000 MGM shares at $24.25 each. The Don's knockout blow was convincing the casino to give him a guarantee that the shares would be bought back at $48.50 when the contract expired. In the wake of the riot in the MGM foyer, Don King helped himself to $30 million. Even the deep Vegas vats had been bruised by the Tyson-King experience.

King still had a slippery grip on the heavyweight division, as he retained the rights to promote Evander Holyfield and Michael Moorer. He matched the pair and Holyfield beat a brave Moorer convincingly, stopping him in the eighth round. The result inside the ropes was satisfying for Evander, putting right the one unavenged blot on his record, but outside, in his pocket, it was less so. The pay-per-view sales were disappointing. People would cough up to watch Tyson fight his way out of a paper bag, but Holyfield's appeal was dictated by the value of his opponent. His next bout was due to be against the lanky Briton Henry Akinwande, but that disintegrated into farce when Akinwande tested positive for a strain of the hepatitis virus a couple of days before the bout. Many believed the machinations of the King of the Dark to be at hand again, when ticket and television sales for the fight were revealed to be almost stagnant. Holyfield shrugged off yet more weirdness in boxing and announced that he would fight Vaughan Bean in a smaller promotion in his home town of Atlanta. He would be watching Tyson's reapplication for his licence with interest.

*   *   *

The King of the Dark had two more tricks up his sleeve, though, even when his repertoire seemed as though it was almost exhausted. He had lost Mike Tyson and he was about to be retried on the fraud charges that we had spoken about in Las Vegas. Frank Warren had broken his cross-Atlantic contract with Don King and announced more court action against him. The vultures seemed to be circling above that shock of electric hair, but King remained endlessly resourceful, innately cunning. He inked an agreement with the British promoter of Lennox Lewis, Frank Maloney, in place of his deal with Warren, and secured himself a slice of the action with the one other bankable heavyweight still fighting. Now, inevitably at some point, Mike Tyson would have to come to him again. And then Don King went to court, to face the wrath of the FBI. Once again he threw those smoke rings of his around the proceedings. Soon the distant events of Julio Cesar Chavez versus Harold Brazier were once again drowned in confusion. Don King walked free, whistling 'Yankee Doodle Dandy' on the courtroom steps as he went.

* * *

Bulging from a wide pinstripe suit, his hair cropped close to his head, Mike Tyson sat in the Hughes Justice Complex before a hearing of the New Jersey State Athletic Commission on 30 July 1998. With him were his lawyer, Anthony Fusco, and a new Team Tyson to give sworn testimony on his behalf: Shelly Finkel, Monica Turner, ex-fighters Chuck Wepner, Bobby Czyz and Tom Patti, psychologist Bert Rotman and Muhammad Siddeeq, a schoolteacher and Tyson's Muslim spiritual adviser.

For three and a half hours, testimony was given on Tyson's behalf. Chuck Wepner, who once went fifteen rounds with Muhammad Ali, said, 'Fighters are not always aware of their actions in the ring. Because of the pressure, you lose control and forget things. He moved into a mental zone and a piece of the street came out in him . . . he made a mistake, but he's changed.' Monica described him as 'an awesome husband' and spoke of how he needed boxing 'and boxing needs him'. Tyson was then questioned for forty-five minutes by the assistant attorney general Michael Hass, when he was constantly pressed to apologise for the bite on Holyfield. He did, several times. Then the tension of the event overcame him again. Asked to read a prepared statement by Anthony Fusco, he snapped, 'I don't want to say it now because I'm angry.'

Fusco jumped in quickly to limit any damage, but Tyson interjected again.

'You know what I mean, man? Aah, why do I have to relive my fucking . . .' he trailed off.

Fusco shoved an arm around Tyson's broad shoulders.

'Relax, relax, Mike. Calm down. Come on Mike,' he pleaded.

Afterwards, Tyson denied that he had lost his temper. 'I never lost my cool,' he told the television cameras. 'I was just expressing my hurt.'

Tyson had made his peace with Evander Holyfield months before. At first, it seemed he might never make plain his regret in person. The pair were due to meet at a benefit organised by Muhammad Ali, but Tyson never showed. Then he called Holyfield 'a couple of times' without reply. But eventually they talked. 'We have spoken,' Holyfield said. 'I have nothing against Mike Tyson.'

With due deference to the deliberations of the New Jersey State Athletic Control Board, who had forty-five days to deliver a verdict on his application, Tyson announced that his next opponent would be Lou Savarese, whom he would fight in the autumn in Atlantic City, back where he started.

* * *

It had seemed to be a new start for Mike Tyson, a chance for him to assert his undoubted independence of spirit. But heavyweight fighting is never as it seems. No one rests easy, especially Don King. After years without one, he gained a licence to promote in Atlantic City. And then he gained even more than that. Less than three weeks after making it, Tyson withdrew his licence application in New Jersey, and returned to the Nevada State Athletic Commission. At his side once again was Don King. A hearing was scheduled for 19 September. Mike Tyson declined to comment. The last word went to the King of the Dark.

'We have a contract . . .'

I thought again of Donald McRae's conversation with the now-unemployed John Horne. Horne had nailed Tyson's plight in two paragraphs in 1996, and it seemed more pertinent than ever.

'Mike Tyson is one of a tiny handful of young black men who have found a way out,' Horne said. 'Look at the trouble he has encountered. Look at the troubles of rappers like Tupac Shakur and Snoop Doggy Dog. Let me tell you what happens. This society, America, creates all these illegitimate black kids who know that, as they grow up, maybe one in a hundred thousand of them will have the opportunity to make something out of their lives. Now, white America's kids will buy the records made by Tupac and Snoop, they'll pay to watch Mike Tyson fight. But there is no enduring love or concern for young black people because there should be a million Tupac Shakurs, a million Snoop Doggy Dogs. They just need the chance. Without that, what hope can they live on?

'But the people in power in this country do not support the likes of Tupac or Snoop – despite their popularity. They castigate them for being negative, for focusing on the violence and prejudice of this society, for telling stories about ghetto life. But before they became famous they were just ignored. They were just part of the voiceless black underclass. It's okay for millions of black kids to live this ghetto life, to be limited, to be jailed, to be murdered. Yet as soon as they start writing about it, as soon as they start rapping about it, making a living out of it, creating something out of their pain and suffering, they are damned. Where's the fairness in that?'

Mike Tyson did remove himself by one step from Don King, although it was obvious that any existence in the rarefied air of $200 million fights meant that he would not elude him forever. A ballsy small-timer named Dan Goosen promoted his come-back bout against Franz Botha. Botha convinced himself that he was doing quite well against Tyson for four rounds, even dropping his hands and prancing around like a flabby Rocky, until he walked onto a right hand that would have dropped a buffalo. The punch is always the last thing to go.

After a minor altercation following a shunt in one of his cars and a trial in which even the complainants spoke up for him, Mike Tyson did a few more months of jailtime at the behest of the American justice system. He planned another comeback for November 1999, with perhaps the last of the dust falling from his comet.

* * *

The course of John Barnwell's life began to lead him away from boxing. He had injured his knee when a concrete stairway collapsed on him at the building where he was caretaker, and it had begun to hinder him quite badly. As a trainer, he had always liked to get into the ring himself to hand down his painful lessons, but his movements were becoming restricted and his weight was rising as he was unable to run. He was hoping for some compensation, but that looked unlikely to be forthcoming.

'I fucking hate it, not being able to get in there, like,' he told me. 'I get real fat, can't get the weight off. I've trained all my life, since I was eleven, and I miss it, you know?'

I didn't see John for a few weeks. He wasn't at the gym and there was no answer from his phone. I finally caught him in, and he told me that he'd been in hospital for almost a month and had nearly died.

'I started feeling really shitty and had the tests, like, and they found out I had really bad blood poisoning, so they brought me in. I was in and out of consciousness, like, and they couldn't stop it happening.'

Eventually, it was discovered that John had a problem with his spleen and would probably have to have it removed. If the operation went ahead, he would never be allowed into a ring again. No one seemed sure as to how much boxing had contributed to his illness.

He was discharged from hospital and began an attritional existence, journeying back to the ward every day for five hours of treatment hooked up to a drip-feed before returning home exhausted. But slowly the steroids began to clean his blood, and the spleenectomy was averted. He was still advised by his doctors not to fight.

'I'll see how it goes,' he said. 'I reckon it'll probably be all right to train. I'll have to. The steroids have bloated me, like.'

He added ruefully, 'It's cost me a fucking lot of money, too. I've cancelled a whole load of gigs.'

John was planning to gig a lot more with his band, and the bookings were coming in. He was also writing songs, fishing, sailing and painting; Mickey Sullivan had told me that John was a talented artist. So John's ordinary-extraordinary life took another turn.

Mickey Sullivan kept himself in good shape at Brian Hills's gym, ready to take a fight 'if the money's right'. We'd still meet and spend hours talking boxing. 'I'm getting myself really fit,' he said, as he stood alone by the heavy bag, dripping with sweat. 'You just can't beat that feeling when you're really sharp, really in shape. I love feeling that way.' Mickey was planning some changes, too, dropping his job as a security guard and undertaking some training to become a motorcycle courier. He also still had steady work on the door of a sports bar in Fulham. Boxing would still give him his kicks, even without John as his regular sparring partner.

Billy Heaney slipped away from view. John spoke with him regularly on the phone, but he didn't come to the gym any more.

'He's really out of shape now,' John reported. 'I don't reckon he'll fight again.' He still worked on the door of the Irish pub, still slogged hard on the roads, but the epic fight against Steve The Hammer seemed likely to be his swansong.

One evening, I had a call from Jimmy 'His Nibbs' Ryan. He had finally found a way out of the Basin. His brother had acquired a small scrap-metal company over in Ireland, and there was work there for a willing man, steady work, and the chance of better things to come.

'I reckon there might be a gym there, too,' Nibbs laughed.

'I'll get it on with that Steve Collins now he's retired. I'm going to give it a good go over there, anyway.'

There was nothing more to keep Jimmy in London, that much was for sure.

In the months after my meeting with Roy Shaw, Lenny McLean published his autobiography, *The Guv'nor*, and he became an unlikely movie star, playing a cameo role in the gangster flick *Lock, Stock and Two Smoking Barrels*. He died soon afterwards. McLean's book and my time with Roy were like a last, late wake-up call for me in unlicensed boxing. It was a world running on pure myth. Two men whose lives had intersected had subsequently refashioned events to suit themselves, and yet I doubted the sincerity of neither. Ultimately, their stories contained much of the mystique of unlicensed fighting, and much of its appeal. And Lenny did Roy one last favour, too. His book proved so popular that his publisher offered Roy a deal of his own. As Lenny had already appropriated their disputed title of 'Guv'nor', Roy called his *Pretty Boy*.

* * *

It felt like an ending of sorts. For their own good reasons, the men in this book were out of the game. They had demonstrated how licensed and unlicensed boxing was a whole, how men slipped between the two, how the will to fight would always exist, however it might be framed and coded. There had been as much savagery at the most lucrative fight of all time as there had been in the rundown gyms and backstreet pubs of south London, and probably more. And yet in those same places there were examples of nearly every great human quality. There was brotherhood and friendship, mutual and unspoken understanding, the endurance of suffering, the discipline of personal achievement, the purity of competition, the facing of fear and the respect for the codes of the sport. There were many little acts of greatness and courage, many personal boundaries crossed and goals superseded, many lives left a little better. Boxing was hard and fierce; this they all knew, accepted and embraced. This was its point. Boxing took lives, but it saved more. To me, abolitionist arguments had become pointless. Some men would always fight, and when they did, they would find out about themselves. Whether they accumulated millions, like Tyson, or nothing, like Nibbs, or John, or Mickey, or Roy, it had shaped their lives. Mike Tyson might still face an ugly end, but it would be no uglier than the one he would have endured without boxing in Brownsville as the bullied boy, no uglier than those of the millions of kids that John Horne spoke of, ignored in their ghettos. John Barnwell's stammer was a handicap that fighting had helped him to overcome, that offered him the chance of a life less ordinary. There was more good than bad here, despite the Dogman and Ray White and the other men who had slipped between the cracks of ordinary life and descended into some other kind of existence all together. Fighting, licensed or not, coded or not, would be around as long as there were men to fight. It was like a slow river rolling, constantly replenished.

*   *   *

On a warm night as winter turned to spring, Brian Hills's gym was empty save for one man pounding out a beat on the heavy bag. It was the hard-hitting, slightly fat middleweight whom I'd seen training at Danny's while waiting for John and Mickey and Billy to show up.

He smiled when I walked in.

'Still thinking about Vegas when you're punching that?'

'Yeah,' he grinned again. He leaned against the bag. 'Vegas, that would do me. Or maybe Madison Square Garden . . .'

He looked away. The buzz of the timer sounded the start of another three minutes. He began to throw some jabs into the well-beaten leather, and the bag started to swing on its chain. He'd soon found his rhythm and the punches started getting harder. A thin smile passed across his face. After a while, they started to sound like music.